From Loss to Life and Back Again

A Curriculum for Grief Groups

Facilitator Guide

Praise for the curriculum:

Cindy's curriculum is remarkable in its clarity of purpose – equipping group participants to cope with their grief as they continue living. The combination of mindfulness, storytelling and education provide opportunity for participation on all levels.

Cathy Payne Anderson(she/her), MDiv, BCC
Clinical Chaplain, Behavioral Health
PERMANENTE MEDICINE

This grief curriculum allows veterans to explore and express their grief in an effective but sensitive manner. The curriculum gives language to the complex emotions that we all go through, no matter where you are in your grief journey. The tools and activities provided not only allow veterans to better understand their own grief but also become more comfortable with the uncomfortable feelings that come with it.

Yun Simpson, LGSW

It was clear and easy to read both the guide and the curriculum, which I think is important. You cited and supported your grief model, and the sessions were based on the literature— which was great. I liked the visuals throughout the curriculum. I feel like the curriculum could be adapted by a counselor, a social worker, or a peer support worker. There's so much more I could say about how much I like this curriculum and the session breakdowns.

Olivia Easley, PhD, FL-LMHC, NC-LCMHC

I think the workbook is amazing. I actually was telling my sister about it, and I'd welcome an e-version!

Veteran participant

From Loss to Life and Back Again

A Curriculum for Grief Groups
Facilitator Guide

Rev. Dr. Cindy R. Wallace, BCC-SP, CCISM, CT

From Loss to Life and Back Again. Facilitator Guide
Facilitator Guide, Paperback ISBN: 9798876522481

Also Available: From Loss to Life and Back Again. Participant Guide
Participant Guide, Paperback ISBN: 9798876523068

Also Available: eBook Participant Guide

Photo and illustration credits:
Cover photo Unknown Author licensed under CC BY-SA
p 16 Ball of Grief, Wright 2023
p 17 Dual Process Model, Stoebe & Schut 2010, 246
p 18 Grief Reactions, Quality of Life Publishing 2013, 2020
p 32 Unknown Author licensed under CC BY
p 41 Spiritual Bypassing, TheMindFool, 2021
p 44 Unknown Author licensed under CC BY-SA-NC

Imprint: Independently published
First Printing 2024
Printed in USA

Dedication

This work is in memory and honor of my loved ones whose lives and deaths have been a guide on my own journey of grief. My Pa-Paw Preacher's death when I was 10 was my first experience of death. I learned it's okay to be sad and laugh at funny memories at the same time. My father's sudden death by heart attack tore my world apart but helped me identify my calling which led me to my career in chaplaincy. My mother's life with Alzheimer's and eventual death taught me patience and compassion for her, myself, and others who experience loss a little at a time. My aunt and sister-in-law's ordeal and death due to breast cancer taught me faith and doubt live hand in hand. My brother's death in a car accident taught me that life can change in a moment, so make the most of every moment you have together.

All these make me who I am and inform what I do.

I miss you all.

Thanks

Thank you to my husband, and children who have loved me through my experience of grief and listened to many stories of grief from my work. Your love and support ground me and fill my life with joy.

Thank you to my friend, Cathy, and my friend and colleague, Carol, who read over this curriculum and gave me feedback. Special thanks to Paul Mouw for his generous work as my editor.

Table of Contents

Pages of the Participant Guide are in blue boxes

About the Cover Image

The image of the changing seasons is the perfect image to illustrate the title of this book: *From Grief to Loss and Back Again*. The changing seasons represent the seasons of life to me. We are born in the spring of our life, blossom and flower into summer, and later begin to slow down and let go of things that no longer serve us in the fall. As time passes our physical body is ready for its rest in order to make space for new growth. This happens over and over again. Unfortunately, winter comes sooner than we want for some and we are thrown into our own emotional winter of grief and loss. But spring always comes with new growth, and summer is just around the corner to let the sun shine down and reenergize us in preparation for the next season of letting go and sitting in the dark stillness of winter again. From grief to loss and back again. It is the way of life. "For everything there is a season, and a time for every matter under heaven . . . ." (Ecclesiastes 3:1).

Preface

This work is the culmination of a lifelong dance with grief. Some of my earliest memories are of my father telling me about his mother, Ola Mae, who died when he was nineteen. His and his sibling's grief for their mother was palpable at family gatherings. Their love for her was timeless and strong, and they kept her love alive in our family to the present day. Though I never met her, I have always felt I knew her.

Long hospital visits, sitting with the dying, and going to funerals were regular practices growing up. When my grandfather died at the hospital when I was ten without being able to see him, I was devastated. He was my world, and I couldn't imagine life without him. That was the first death experience that shattered my world.

My family has since lived through multiple losses from cancer, accidents, old age, suicide, miscarriage, Alzheimer's, and heart attacks. Some deaths were sudden and unexpected, and others were long and drawn out with us praying for relief from their pain and release from this world. Each experience was grounded in support from family, friends, church family, and the small community that banded together to take care of each other when times were tough. People showed up with food and hugs, and they stayed to wash dishes, make coffee, and make sure everyone had whatever they needed.

This was my context. Pastoral care was nurtured and the skills of being present were honed. It was after my father died unexpectedly in 2002 that I found chaplaincy. Within it, I found ministry with people at the darkest times of life and the raw moments of grief and loss. I finally felt at home in ministry and have been companioning others on the journey of grief ever since.

Acknowledgements

I have been supported by so many people in this process, but by none more than my husband, Rob, who is my biggest fan, my partner, my best friend, and the love of my life. Thank you for everything.

My boss and friend, Carol Ramsey-Lucas, pushed what was already spinning around in my head into fruition with the goal of creating this curriculum in real time. She provided the time I needed to research, write, experiment, edit, and edit, and edit some more. She read through the curriculum, led groups, and provided feedback to make it so much better. Thank you!

Cathy Anderson, my sweet friend. Our friendship was forged in the fires of Clinical Pastoral Education and has burned brightly in my heart ever since. She also encouraged me to write this curriculum so she could use it, too! She was my first, second, and third reader, offering valuable insights catching mistakes, and helping make the curriculum what it has become. Mwah!

To Paul Mouw who graciously served as my copy editor and helped me think through parts of this project I never would have thought of on my own—thank you! thank you!

To my colleagues who have agreed to walk with me on this journey of grief work-thank you. It is a difficult road, holding the painful stories of people month after month. Thank you for your dedication and diligence.

To the veterans who have attended our grief groups—thank you for being vulnerable enough to share your stories with us. We hold your stories with gratitude, grace, and dignity. We respect you and care for you and your loved ones more than you will ever know. This work is for you.

Introduction for Facilitators

This curriculum was initially created for use in a 6-week virtual group for veterans experiencing loss due to the death of a loved one, though the principles discussed have broader application than this specific setting. It is written to be expanded to an 8-week curriculum if desired. If using it as a 6-week, you can choose which 6 sessions fit your group best. You can utilize information from the other sessions to enhance the discussion in the chosen session. My personal choice would be to choose to use either session 3 about family dynamics or session 4 about identity and then incorporate parts of one into the other. My other choice would be to use either session 4 about Trauma and Grief or session 5 on spirituality and grief. Working with veterans I tend to use the trauma and grief session more and incorporate spirituality into the session on resilience as a strong spiritual foundation is shown in research to build resilience.

This curriculum is designed to address issues related to normal and traumatic grief. It incorporates concepts from George Bonnano, Holly Prigerson, Robert Neimeyer, William Worden, Collin Murry Parkes, John Bowlby, Thomas Attig, Erich Lindemann's symptomatology of acute grief, Mitchell and Anderson's ideas of relationship loss, and Janice Nadeau and Ester Shapiro's theories of grief as a family process. Though often taken out of context, it is difficult to argue the influence Elizabeth Kùbler-Ross' five stages of grief has had in our society's understanding of the bereavement process. Grief does not occur in a linear fashion nor does it progress in prescribed stages or phases, as Kubler-Ross herself stated in her joint work with David Kessler, *On Grief and Grieving: Finding the Meaning of Grief Through the Five Stages of Loss*. David Kessler's recent *Finding Meaning: The Sixth Stage of Grief* also influence thoughts in this curriculum. Lucy Pone's work on resilient grieving and Megan Divine's practical coping strategies are heavily represented throughout the curriculum as well, along with multiple other resources that serve as the research framework for the grief curriculum.

This curriculum is intended to be used for people deemed appropriate for a group setting. A bereavement assessment should be used to determine the nature of the grief, how recently the death has occurred, and if the bereaved needs individual support prior to attending a group. It is recommended that the bereaved person be 2-3 months past the death prior to attending a group. To address more chronic or complicated grief, the DSM-5-TR and the ICD 11 include a diagnosis of Prolonged Grief Disorder (PGD) and distinguishes it from Major Depressive Disorder (MDD), generalized anxiety disorder (GAD), and post-traumatic stress disorder (PTSD). The full criteria may be found in either manual, however, it is important to note that Criterion A states the death must be at least 12 months ago for adults and at least 6 months ago for children and adolescents. Symptoms include intense yearning/longing for the deceased and preoccupation with memories of the deceased nearly every day for at least the last month. Other symptoms that may be clinically significant include identity disruption, sense of disbelief about the death, avoidance of reminders of the death, intense emotional pain, difficulty reintegrating back into activities and relationships, and numbness (Prigerson, et al., 2021, 112). Only licensed mental health professionals can assess and diagnose a person with PGD, but all clinicians must be aware of the signs and symptoms to refer people for appropriate help.

Through mindful grounding practices, psychoeducation, process questions, activities, and homework assignments participants begin to engage their grief reactions and adapt to their new reality. Coping strategies will be introduced to help manage complicated grief reactions (Supiano and Luptak, 2013). There are 8 different group topics including:

- Grief Orientation and Introduction,
- Acceptance,
- Family Matters: How our Attachments Affect our Grief
- Identity: Who Am I Now?
- Trauma and grief,
- Spirituality and Grief,
- Expressing Grief: Lament and Hope,
- Resilience and Meaning-Making.

Pre-Group Screening and Orientation

Once the referral has been received, an interview will take place to assess appropriateness for the group. Within this interview the needs, expectations, and commitment to the group will be discussed. If further assessment is needed, the Inventory of Complicated Grief will be administered (Prigerson et al., 1995). The assessment can be accessed at https://psychology-tools.com/test/inventory-complicated-grief. It will score the assessment instantly.

To conclude the screening interview, a summary of the purpose, logistics, expectations, and rationale for the group will take place. Prospective group members should be encouraged to ask questions to further assess their alignment with the group.

Leader Characteristics and Traits

"You don't have to be larger than life to help people in the darkest moments of their lives…[but it does require that] we listen athletically, with one's whole attention, and it is physically exhausting. It feels like a contact sport" (Ackerman, 1997, 285). The ideal characteristics and traits for a leader of a grief group should include an individual who is empathetic, caring, and a good communicator. An ideal group leader will be able to provide emotional support, manage group dynamics, provide clarity, and offer hope for the group members. As a leader, the individual should have the ability to motivate and engage their group members, comfort, and at times challenge them.

Group Goals

The goals for the grief group are as follows:

- Provide psychoeducation on the grief process.

- Provide emotional support to group members through their loss.

- Validate each person's unique grief process.

- Discuss coping skills to help participants manage the daily impact of grief.

Tips

- This was created as a virtual group and therefore the bereaved person's phone number and email address were necessities in making the group work well. Some participants with no email or access to virtual applications called in to the group or were called in by the facilitator.

- A reminder email was sent the day of the group and a few minutes before the group started. This helped those experiencing brain fog from grief to remember to join the group at the correct time.

- You will notice a few of the homework assignments have an optional shorter assignment. Since the participants are in different places on their grief journey, I found it helpful to have a shorter, less intense option for the more recently bereaved.

- It is vital to have a cadre of referral resources available as some people will need individual counseling, groups that occur at different times of day/night, or specific grief needs (loss of child, perinatal loss, suicide loss). Check with your local hospice organization as they often have the most comprehensive grief support offering.

Evaluation

Provide group members with an evaluation after the last group session. I used Survey Monkey and created an evaluation asking for general feedback on how helpful the group was for the participant as well as specific feedback regarding which topics and which homework assignments were most helpful.

Follow-Up

This group is meant to be a beginning point in engaging the grief process. Some participants may require individual support to continue their grief work and others may require other outside referrals. We offer an ongoing monthly check-in group as a way for participants to participate in aftercare. Others may feel prepared to continue their journey of grief through re-engagement in personal relationships and activities. It is important to remember that grief is a normal part of life and is an ongoing process. Additional losses and difficult life transitions may trigger intense grief reactions, necessitating further follow-up.

Session 1: Grief Orientation and Group Introduction Facilitator Review

Background Information

The idea of a "grief work theory" was first proposed in Sigmund Freud's work *Mourning and Melancholia* in which he stated the function of grief was "to detach thoughts and feelings from the dead person so that the bereaved person can move on with his or her life" (Archer, 2008, 45). In the 1940's the term "grief work" was coined by psychiatrist Erich Lindemann in his research working with survivors of the Coconut Grove tragedy. His work influenced later grief theorists providing a list of common symptoms of grief including somatic distress, preoccupation with images of the deceased, guilt, hostile reactions, and disruption in patterns of conduct (Williams, 2014). Colin Murray Parkes later described grief as a process that includes numbness, pining for the deceased, disorganization, and despair before recovering. He noted that part of the grief process includes "painful repetitious recollection of the loss experience" that leads to acceptance of the loss (Parkes, 1986, 95). Parkes notes that throughout the process the bereaved experiences longing for the deceased that leads to a restless searching for their loved one in hopes of finding the lost person. This preoccupation with the lost person is often lived out in anxiety, busyness, and a disorganized state of being. The goal of grief work is to establish a reorganization "gaining a new identity" with a "new set of expectations and roles" (Parkes, 2986, 93).

Grief is holistic, meaning it affects us emotionally, physically, cognitively, behaviorally, and spiritually (Doka and Chow, 2021, 235-241). The Grief Reactions page provides an overview of how grief affects us in these areas. Grief is as unique as each individual who experiences it. No one person grieves the exact same as the next. There is no right or wrong way to grieve (Doka and Chow, 2021, 241). I tell people that as long as you are not hurting yourself or someone else and the property you damage is your own, then everything else is on the table when it comes to grief reactions. Obviously, this statement is meant to normalize grief reactions. It is not a means of true assessment. The Traffic Light Reactions page can help group members assess what level of care they may need.

There is no timetable for grief. Grief is not linear. What grief specialists refer to as "early grief" is the first two years of grief. If the death was sudden or traumatic, or if the deceased was a child this timeline may be extended up to the first five years. Grief is not something you "get over." Grief stays with us all our lives because we are grieving the loss of a person who cannot be replaced. We learn how to manage our grief and to connect with the spirit of our loved one (Doka and Chow, 2021, 241, 251-254).

This curriculum is built on the idea of Stroebe and Schutt's dual process model of grief that states people move back and forth between focusing on the loss and resuming daily activities. The dual process model posits that the bereaved person oscillates between loss-orientation and resto-ration-orientation. Stroebe and Schut describe loss-orientation as "the bereaved person's concen-tration on, appraising and processing of some aspect of the loss experience itself" (2010, 277). This can include a painful longing for the lost person, even to the point of searching for the de-ceased person. Restoration-orientation focuses on "secondary stressors" that result from the loss that includes "struggling to reorient oneself in a changed world without the deceased person" (Stroebe and Schut, 2010, 277). Over time there is more attention given to restoration-oriented tasks than loss-oriented tasks as coping skills are incorporated and the bereaved forms a new identity (Stroebe and Schut, 2010, 283).

Dual Process Model of Coping with Bereavement
Stroebe & Schut, 2010, 276

The curriculum is also influenced by Robert Kastenbaum's theory that grief comes in waves demonstrating "distress does not end with the first wave of shock and grief" but ebbs and flows after "the realization that life is supposed to go on" (Bonnano, 2019, 63). Some waves you see coming, like holidays, anniversaries, birthdays, and can plan rituals to mark the time as you see fit. Other waves sneak up and crash over you when you least expect it—the smell in the grocery store, the tears in the middle of the meeting, the song on the radio.

Studies show that grieving people need safe spaces to share their grief experience with others. The experience of universality found in grief groups helps to build trust and cohesion between group members and has been proven to be a helpful source of support especially when dealing with traumatic grief (Cacciatore, et al., 2021). Bereavement groups are one of the most common types of professional grief support. Professionally guided bereavement groups are suited to help avoid social isolation which is a risk factor in developing prolonged grief disorder. Studies report grieving individuals value the "social nature of the group experience." Other advantages of a bereavement group are the development of coping strategies, instilling hope, normalization of grief reactions, and social support for dealing with difficult social interactions after the loss (Maass, et al., 2022).

Many mourners can effectively cope with their loss in time; however, approximately 10% of mourners develop Prolonged Grief Disorder (PGD) (Maass, et al., 2022). Studies show that violent death often hinders the ability of the bereaved to make meaning of the loss which can increase symptoms of PGD (Boelen, 2019). Other symptoms of PGD include intense yearning, avoidance, disbelief, and intrusive and disturbing thoughts about the death. Some bereaved may show signs of disconnection from daily life and in some cases suicidal thoughts. Other factors associated with PGD are perceived lack of support, poor coping skills, substance use, history of mental illness, and death of a child (Waller, et al., 2016). Most people experiencing PGD also tend to struggle to accept the reality of the death, express bitterness, and experience perceived meaninglessness in life. These symptoms often become so severe they impede social and occupational functioning (Supiano and Luptak, 2013). While the intention of this group is not to diagnose, as stated earlier, it is recommended that the facilitator be aware of symptoms of Prolonged Grief Disorder as found in the DSM V-TR for referral purposes.

Session 1: Grief Orientation and Group Introduction

From Page 19, Participant Guide

Goals

- Introduce ourselves and identify what brings each person to the group and what they hope for themselves at the end of the group.

- Establish group rules for the sessions.

- Learn about the nature of grief and discuss participant's experiences.

Objectives

- Participants will begin to form initial bonds and establish group rules.

- Participants will learn typical grief responses from emotional, cognitive, physical, spiritual, and behavioral perspectives.

- Participants will be invited to discuss their personal experience of grief.

Group Rules

Each session we will go over our group rules to remind us of expectations during the group meetings. These are rules that help us build psychological safety into the group. Please feel free to share other rules you believe would be helpful.

1. Confidentiality: Group topics stay within group time. The facilitators are mandated reporters and will have to report any suicidal thoughts, homicidal thoughts/threats, and child elder abuse as part of our safety protocols. Beyond those issues, it is expected that both facilitators and participants maintain confidentiality about the things discussed in the group setting.

2. Respect: Do not interrupt or talk over each other. Do not engage in conversations while a topic is being discussed. Allow everyone an opportunity to speak.

20   From Loss to Life and Back Again

3. Engagement: Active participation is expected during group sessions. The group develops and grows when everyone participates.

4. Communication: Speak from an "I" perspective. Do not assume to know what others are thinking and do not speak for anyone but yourself.

Mindfulness Exercise

Each session we will begin with an activity to prepare us for our group setting. To begin, place feet on the floor and put hands in a comfortable position. Take a couple of deep breaths at your own pace. If you feel safe doing so, close your eyes; otherwise, lower your gaze. Participants are invited to settle into the present moment by noticing where we are and allowing us to be in the here and now. We will focus on our breathing and bringing our thoughts back to the here and now for a few minutes, then we will return to the group. Today, we will begin with a grounding exercise that asks: "Where are you?" and "What time is it?" The answers to those questions are "here" and "now" (Coenen, 2020, p.74). After grounding exercise, we will be invited to share our names, a little about what brings us to the group, and what we hope to accomplish.

Check-in

The Big Ball of Grief is one tool we use to help us identify what we may be currently feeling as part of our grief process (Wright 2003). The ball is made up of a tangle of different words representing some of the emotions experienced during grief. Often, we associate sadness or despair with grief, but there are many other emotions we may not realize that occur as well. The Big Ball of Grief illustrates how the different emotions flow together, sometimes becoming tangled up with others along the way and showing how we often feel multiple emotions at once. Some words occur more than once because some feelings may come up more often than others. Naming the emotions helps us untangle the chaos and make sense of why we are so exhausted, frustrated, and confused. When we understand ourselves better, we can then be more compassionate with ourselves on this journey.

- Are there any emotions that you see that resonate with you?

- Are there emotions that you don't see that you experience?

- Are you surprised by any of these emotions?

The Big Ball of Grief
(Wright, 2003)

22   From Loss to Life and Back Again

Psychoeducation

Grief is a normal reaction to loss. We experience loss when a loved one dies, but also during life transitions where our roles change, during health crises, when a relationship ends, or from job loss or retirement. There is no right or wrong way to grieve. Everyone experiences grief differently. Grief is not linear and does not follow a stage or phase. It ebbs and flows like waves. Some waves you see coming, like holidays, anniversaries, and birthdays. Others sneak up and crash over you—the smell in the grocery store, the tears in the middle of the meeting, the song on the radio. There is no timeline for our grief. What grief specialists refer to as "early grief" is the first two years of grief. Grief stays with us all our lives because we are grieving the loss of a person who cannot be replaced. We learn how to manage our grief and to connect with the spirit of our loved one. Typically, people move back and forth between focusing on the loss and resuming daily activities (Stroebe & Schut, 2010, 276).

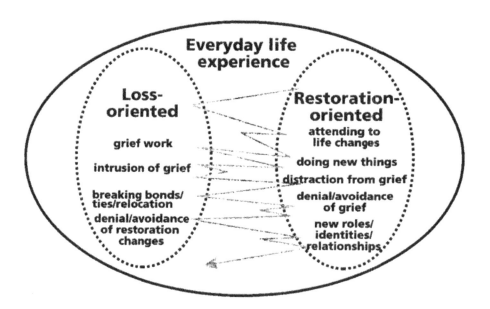

Dual Process Model of Coping with Bereavement
(Stroebe & Schut, 2010, 276)

Process Question

Grief affects us in many ways: emotionally, cognitively, spiritually, behaviorally, and physically. The chart below offers a brief list of grief responses. What have you experienced in your grief process?

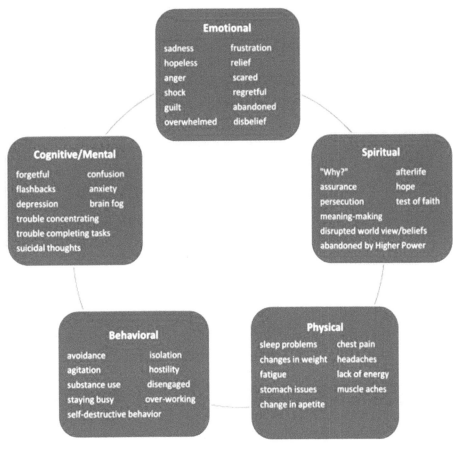

Grief Reactions
(adapted from Quality of Life Publishing Co, 2013,2020)

24   From Loss to Life and Back Again

Activities

Sometimes it's hard to tell if we are managing our grief well or if it is getting worse. While each of us grieves in our own unique way, there are signs that tell us when we need more help. Grief will be painful, but we need to be aware of our limits. Using the traffic light, circle the grief reactions you have experienced recently.

Traffic Light Reactions

Panic attacks

Trouble with daily activities (hygiene, work, paying bills, eating, sleeping)

Isolation

Hopelessness/meaninglessness

Suicidal thoughts/wishing to die

Mood swings

Nightmares

Guilt

Eating/sleeping irregularly

Pain is overwhelming

Disconnected

Managing intense emotions

Feeling connected

Eating/sleeping enough

Advocating for yourself

Acceptance of circumstances

Session 1: Grief Orientation and Group Introduction 25

Homework

- Use the Big Ball of Grief to check-in with yourself and your feelings this week.

- Create personalized survival rules for grieving. Think of the things that you need in order to get through the day and then create a list or chart. Take a photo and keep it in your phone for quick reference. Use the "My Grief Guide" to create your list.

My Grief Guide

"Grief erupts into life and rearranges everything" (Devine, 2021, 16). Nothing is the same anymore and everything takes more energy and effort than you have to give. Some days you feel lonely and some days you want to be alone. In this new landscape of your life, think about what helps you get through each minute, hour, and day. I've added 2 things to get you started. What do you need others to understand while you are grieving right now?

- **Eat something-you feel better when you eat something good for you.**

- **Move your body-even if it's just to stretch.**

Session 2: Acceptance
Facilitator Review

Background Information

This session is built on William Worden's task model of grief. Task One is acceptance of the reality of the loss. Acceptance is necessary for the individual to begin to manage their grief reactions. This involves both cognitive acceptance and emotional acceptance and is a process that may be revisited throughout the grief process (Worden et al., 2021,273). Part of this process is acknowledging the ways in which your life has changed externally, internally, and spiritually.

Changes to daily life functions are external adjustments. This might include learning to cook for one, having to take care of the bills and house responsibilities, becoming a single parent, or losing the person for whom one would normally provide care. Internal adjustments refer to how the death has affected the griever's sense of self and identity. This may include questioning, "Who am I, if not a [parent, spouse, sibling, partner, child, caregiver]?" Some grievers express they feel part of themselves died with their loved one. Spiritual adjustments refer to how the death shatters an individual's beliefs about the world, their Higher Power, or their connectedness to their spirituality. People may find themselves asking "Why me? Why my loved one? Why now?" Individuals may feel as though they are being punished or abandoned by God/Higher Power and begin to question everything they have trusted about the goodness of God/Higher Power/or life in general. Others may find a source of strength and hope from their spirituality (Worden, et al, 2021, 273).

The activity in this session will explore what gets in the way of acceptance by asking the participants to explore their own "what if" and "if only" questions. These questions are built on the belief that something they did or did not do would have kept their loved alive. In most instances, this is not true, so it is another reality they must learn to accept. In some cases, the individual may determine that an action taken at the appropriate time could have prevented or postponed the death event, and there may be a hint of truth to that belief. The belief does not have to be logical to wreak havoc. The reality is, no amount of questioning ourselves will change the outcome. Continuing the question is choosing to torment ourselves with guilt and shame that keeps us stuck in the grief process. Doka and Chow state, "Persons can feel guilty over things that they could not really control" (2021, 239). The goal of the activity is to name the questions that they have been going over in their mind, take a moment to check the validity of those thoughts, and accept that their current reality remains, no matter the thoughts.

Session 2: Acceptance

From Page 27, Participant Guide

Goals

- Discuss acceptance and identify what blocks the work of acceptance.

- Improve self-compassion and mindfulness.

- Recognize and discuss practical solutions to daily changes.

Objectives

- Participants will give themselves permission to begin accepting the reality of their loss and the resulting life changes.

- Participants will learn to embrace the present and begin looking forward to the future.

Group Rules

Take a moment to review the group rules we established in the initial session. These build psychological safety for our sessions.

1. Confidentiality: Group topics stay within group time. The facilitators are mandated reporters and will have to report any suicidal thoughts, homicidal thoughts/threats, and child elder abuse as part of our safety protocols. Beyond those issues, it is expected that both facilitators and participants maintain confidentiality about the things discussed in the group setting.

2. Respect: Do not interrupt or talk over each other. Do not engage in conversations while a topic is being discussed. Allow everyone an opportunity to speak.

3. Engagement: Active participation is expected during group sessions. The group develops and grows when everyone participates.

4. Communication: Speak from an "I" perspective. Do not assume to know what others are thinking and do not speak for anyone but yourself.

Mindfulness Exercise: 5-4-3-2-1 Grounding Meditation

The purpose of this exercise is to place yourself in the here and now. With feet flat on the floor, hands on your lap, sitting upright to facilitate deep breaths, take a couple of cleansing breaths and begin.

- Look for 5 things you can see. Notice the textures, color, shapes.

- Find 4 things you can touch. Reach out and touch these items, noticing how different they feel from each other.

- Notice 3 things you hear. Listen without judgment. Listen to what is present in the stillness.

- Find 2 things you smell. Smell your coffee, cologne, lotion, candle, etc.

- Notice 1 thing you can taste. Take a sip of water, coffee, tea, or take a bite of peppermint or gum.

- Allow yourself to stay in the present moment for a few seconds. Repeat any of the steps that help you stay present. Then notice the weight of your body in the chair, your feet on the floor and when you're ready open your eyes and return to the room (Pikörn, n.d.).

Check-in

The group facilitator should check in using the Big Ball of Grief (From Session 1, Page 21) to ask how each participant is experiencing their grief today (Wright, 2003). Ask participants to share a rule they came up with for their "My Rules for Surviving Grief" list.

Psychoeducation

Acceptance is an ongoing work in the grief process. We are faced with the work of acceptance when we pick up the phone to call our loved one, only to remember he or she is gone. Denial and avoidance are ways we instinctively try to protect ourselves from the pain of loss. However, denying the reality of the loss only prolongs the grief, thus causing more intense suffering. A healthier way to address our loss is to acknowledge the losses we are experiencing in the wake of our loved one's death. The primary loss is the physical presence of your loved one, but there are secondary losses: your dreams for the future, your concept of safety and security upon realizing this can happen to you, your financial security, your sense of identity in relation to your loved one, and a loss of routine that comes with upheaval.

Slowly, one step at a time, we learn to adapt to our life changes. (Iglewicz, et al., 2019) Acceptance does not mean you're OK with what occurred; however, it does mean you begin to re-construct your life in the aftermath of the loss. You will learn new ways of connecting with the memories, the dreams, and the presence of your loved one in meaningful ways. You'll begin to feel more comfortable reaching out to family members and friends to reduce isolation. Practicing self-compassion, caring for physical needs, and engaging in mean-ing-making activities can help in the work of acceptance.

Process Questions

- Describe 1-2 life changes you have experienced since the death of your loved one.

- What are some of the secondary losses you are experiencing?

- What does acceptance mean for you?

- What gets in the way of acceptance?

Activities

One aspect of grief that delays acceptance is ruminating over the "what if" and "if only" questions that arise. When your loved one dies, your mind searches for ways to make sense of the loss. This exercise is a reality check for those questions. Use the Reality Check on the next page to explore your "what if" and "if only" statements. After talking through these statements, try rewording your statements to use the phrase "even if." Does this offer a different perspective about the circumstances of the death (Coenen, 2020)?

- What part of the story have you been telling yourself that is not completely true?

- Are you holding yourself or someone else accountable even though the outcome may not have changed?

- Are you holding on to things that were actually out of your control?

- Can you release that part?

It is a normal process during grief to think back about your loved one's death and wonder if there might be a different outcome "if only I had… (insert your thought here)." The "what if" questions and "if only" statements are our way of trying to make sense of the death. It is how we work toward acceptance of the reality we are facing. However, continuing to focus on what might have happened for too long can keep us stuck in our grief. Naming the questions and talking them through can help us release emotions tied to them and better accept our realities. (Adapted from Coenen, 2020, 76-77)

Write down your "what if" and "if only" statements. Then, try rewriting them using the phrase "even if." Notice what changes with the rewrite. What emotions come up for you?

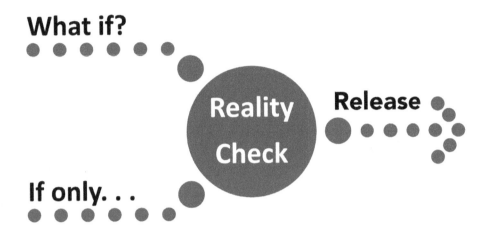

Meditation Practice

Place your feet flat on the floor, place your hands in a comfortable position, and sit up so that you can breathe easily. If you feel safe to close your eyes, please do so. Take a few deep breaths to settle you. Place your hands in front of you and on the inhale imagine you are picking up the things that are keeping you stuck—the things that are out of your control. Hold them in your hands while holding your breath for 2 counts, then throw them away from you on your exhale. With each exhale, release the "what ifs," the "if onlys," and stories that are not true. Do this 2-3 times, then take a couple of deep breaths to settle yourself before returning to the room.

Homework

- Write a letter to your loved one who has passed. Within that letter, express everything you want to tell them, including the pain their death has caused you, the changes in your life, and how you are managing it all. Allow this writing exercise to be a form of emotional release. Next week, we will take the time to share how writing the letter made you feel. You will not be asked to read your letter to the group.

- If writing a letter to your loved one feels too intense, then try this exercise: Everybody has something about themselves they don't like; something that causes them to feel insecure or not "good enough" (i.e., an unhealthy habit, a physical attribute, or a way of relating to others). During grief, you may experience feelings of guilt, shame, anger or frustration with yourself or others that may come out as self-criticism. When you notice that you are being unnecessarily critical toward yourself, the following exercise can help to cultivate a more compassionate, encouraging voice.

From a Friend to Yourself:

- Think about a friend who is wise, loving and compassionate. Imagine that this friend can see all your strengths and weaknesses, including what you don't like about yourself. This friend is kind, accepting, and forgiving.

- Write a letter to yourself from the perspective of this friend, focusing on the perceived inadequacy for which you tend to judge yourself. What would this friend say to you from the perspective of unlimited compassion? And if you think this friend would suggest possible changes you should make, how might these suggestions embody feelings of care, encouragement, and support?

- After writing the letter, put it down for a little while. Then come back to the letter and read it again, really letting the words sink in. Feel the compassion as it pours into you, soothing and comforting you. Love, connection, and acceptance are your birthright. To claim them you need only to look within yourself (Neff, n.d.).

Session 2: Acceptance 33

Session 3: Family Matters: How our Attachments Affect our Grief Facilitator Review

Background Information

John Bowlby's work on attachment theory in the 1960's is the foundation upon which grief work is built. Current grief theories, including the Stroebe & Schut's Dual Process Model substantiate the importance of understanding a client's attachment style when providing grief care (Worden, et al., 2021, 270-271). Bowlby's research focused on the importance of the attachment of children to their parents/caregivers. They found when a child is separated from their parents/caregivers and feels a loss of connection, they protest with the hope of restoring connection. In a healthy system, when the child protests, a caring, dependable adult responds to restore connection building a secure attachment for the child to be able to return to play and positive interaction. If the child protests and there is no response, or if the response is inconsistent and unreliable, the child either persists in the protest or in some cases withdraws into despair. This creates an insecure attachment that becomes anxious, clinging to the caregiver or avoidant, suppressing outward reactions to distress. A third type of attachment is disorganized attachment, which is associated with early abuse or neglect and results in erratic behavior often mimicking the behavior of the caregiver. These patterns are believed to continue into adulthood (Worden, et al., 2021, 268-269).

Whether securely or insecurely attached, the individual's behavior reflects their internal state of being. Individuals with secure attachment from childhood learn behavioral flexibility and learn to trust that when they are in need, those needs will be met. In times of distress securely attached adults tend to adapt quicker and experience lower levels of anxiety and avoidance behaviors (Schenck et al., 2016). Individuals with an insecure attachment style tend to become more anxious in times of distress, avoidant – withdrawing from others who could potentially help, or become co-dependent upon an individual who does help (Schenck et al., 2016).

Bowlby's collaboration with Collin Murray Parkes identified patterns in the relationship between attachment security and grief responses. Parkes researched how insecure attachment led to complications in the grief process. Together they posited four phases of mourning: shock and numbness, yearning and searching for the lost loved one, disorganization and despair, and reorganization.

Once through the shock and numbness mourners pine for their loved one, then begin to question their identity and their ability to survive the grief until they are slowly able to put the pieces of their lives together and move forward in a new reality (Worden, et al., 2021, 268-269).

Grief does not happen in a vacuum, rather it causes disruptions to the family unit. Mitchell and Anderson state we all belong to interactional systems with established patterns and functions performed in particular ways by particular people. They write, "When those functions disappear . . . the system as a whole, as well as its individual members may experience a systemic loss" (Mitchell and Anderson, 1983, 44-45). Parkes, Nadeau, and Shapiro all agree that a death forces a change in the roles of the family system. Naduau states, "Individual grief is profoundly shaped by the family context in which it occurs, and the grief of an individual often has profound effects on the family" (2008, 513). Grief is a relational process that impacts the family development creating "a crisis of attachment and a crisis of identity for family members" (Shapiro, 1994, 10). Bonnano writes, "People take on new roles, lose old ones, find new sides to their relationships, and revitalize old sides" (2019, 50-51). As the family grieves their loss, there is an unspoken desire to reestablish stability to support normal family functioning. "Family members responsively adapt to each other's attempts to control overwhelming emotions, reestablish stable patterns of daily living and relating, and reconstruct a sense of self" (Shapiro, 1994, 14).

Grief is also affected by culture. Cultures vary in their expectations of how grief is expressed, what rituals need to take place, and whether the grief process is an individual or communal experience. Spiritual and religious beliefs may also have an affect on how the individual and family talk about death and the afterlife and the rituals performed. Some Western religions focus on judgment and a literal afterlife where many Eastern religions believe in the reincarnation of souls (Doka and Chow, 2021, 245).

In the homework for this week, the participants will be asked to think back to their first experience of death in their family of origin and contemplate the messages about death, dying, and grief they received from their family. They will complete a handout that asks them what they learned, what is still helpful to them, and what would they change about those beliefs. It is important for the facilitator to do this exercise as well to understand the exercise and participate in your own personal reflection.

Session 3: Family Matters—How Our Attachments Affect Our Grief

From Page 33, Participant Guide

Goals

- Learn how attachment styles and relationship quality can affect grief reactions.

- Identify how grief has affected the family structure.

Objectives

- Participants will identify the nature of the attachment to their deceased loved one.

- Participants will identify how changes in their family are affecting their own grief experience.

- Participants will identify sources of supportive relationships in their lives.

Group Rules

Take a moment to review the group rules we established in the initial session. These build psychological safety for our sessions.

1. Confidentiality: Group topics stay within group time. The facilitators are mandated reporters and will have to report any suicidal thoughts, homicidal thoughts/threats, and child elder abuse as part of our safety protocols. Beyond those issues, it is expected that both facilitators and participants maintain confidentiality about the things discussed in the group setting.

2. Respect: Do not interrupt or talk over each other. Do not engage in conversations while a topic is being discussed. Allow everyone an opportunity to speak.

3. Engagement: Active participation is expected during group sessions. The group develops and grows when everyone participates.

4. Communication: Speak from an "I" perspective. Do not assume to know what others are thinking and do not speak for anyone but yourself.

Mindfulness Exercise

Close your eyes, place your arms in a comfortable position and your feet flat on the floor. Turn your attention to your breathing. Try belly breathing with the belly expanding as you inhale and contracting as you exhale. Try to make the exhale last twice as long as the inhale by pretending you are breathing out through a straw. Inhale for 4 counts and exhale for 8 counts. After about three minutes, open your eyes and return to the group.

Check-in

Check in with the group about last week's homework. What was it like to write the letter to your loved one or to yourself? What did you learn about yourself and your situation?

Psychoeducation

When we are born, we seek attachment to a reliable caregiver who can fulfill our needs and protect us when we are unable to care for and protect ourselves. If our needs are met in infancy and childhood, we develop a secure attachment style in our relationships. This results in our learning to trust that when we are in need, those needs will be met. In times of distress, securely attached adults tend to adapt more quickly and experience lower levels of anxiety and avoidance behaviors (Schenck et al., 2016).

If our needs in infancy and childhood are not consistently met, we develop an insecure attachment style. This means that when we are in need, we have no assurance those needs will be met. Adults with an insecure attachment style tend to become more anxious in times of distress. They may become more avoidant—withdrawing from others who could potentially help—or becoming co-dependent upon an individual who does help (Schenck et al., 2016).

Session 3: Family Matters—How Our Attachents Affect Our Grief   35

Grief is a normal response to the loss of an attachment figure/important person in your life. People with insecure attachment styles tend to struggle more with grief and experience complicated grief reactions. This is especially true if the deceased loved one was their primary attachment figure, like a parent, partner, or child (Schenck et al., 2016). The quality of the relationship with the deceased can determine the severity of the grief reactions. Grief reactions may be more severe if the relationship with the deceased is positive and supportive or even was conflicted leaving behind unfinished business (Smigelsky et al., 2020). Some severe grief reactions include intense longing for the deceased, lack of acceptance of the loss, numbness, bitterness, anger, or a loss of meaning. Some reactions may last longer than 6 months, with impairment to daily activities (Maccallum, 2018).

Process Questions

- How would you describe your relationship with your loved one?
- How does the nature of that relationship affect your grief reactions?

Psychoeducation

Grief occurs "in the context of family" (Breen et al., 2019, 174). Each person in the family grieves in his or her unique way. Family structure, social expectations, traditions, and culture all influence the grief process. Loss brings changes in the overall functioning, communication, organization, and internal relations within the family (Özcan & Maya, 2019).

Imagine your family as a mobile—the kind hanging over a baby's bed. As the mobile turns around, all the items move in a rhythm. What happens if we remove one of the items? (It flops sideways, doesn't move around in a circle, stops moving, etc.) Like that mobile, when a person in your family unit dies, the family unit doesn't function as smoothly.

Family roles shift, communication breaks down, and family members act out of their stress and grief.

Process Questions

- How has grief impacted your family?

- What changes have you noticed since the death?

Activities

One way to cope with loss is by reaching out to others for support. However, sometimes people don't know what to say or do and become uncomfortable with our grief. When people are uncomfortable with the pain of others, they will sometimes avoid people who are grieving or will say something awkward to fill the silence that comes with loss and pain. Unfortunately, these awkward statements are not helpful and may even be upsetting to you. Some examples are:

- God needed them more than you did.

- They're in a better place.

- You are young; you can remarry/have another child, etc.

- They wouldn't want you all upset like this.

People say these things because they feel helpless. They want to do something to fix your pain, but there is nothing to be done, so they alleviate their own discomfort instead. One thing we can do when we grieve is to tell people what we need. Together we're going to create a What I Need chart to be able to give to others who ask, "What I Need?"

- Who is someone who has shown up for you?

- Who is someone you could count on to give you what you need?

Think about what you need right now. What would you like someone to say to you? What do you wish someone would do for you? Is there something you wish someone would ask you about? Write your answers below.

Session 3: Family Matters—How Our Attachents Affect Our Grief   37

What I need...

to hear...	someone to do...	to be asked...

Homework

Think back to your first experience of grief and loss in your family of origin. What was the message you received about death and grief? Was it something your family talked about? What traditions did your family have around death and grief? Use the "Grief Is…" handout on the next page to think through your former and current beliefs about grief and loss. Below is one sample.

What I learned…

- Everyone dies. Death is normal. You're expected to go to the funeral home for visitation, take food to the family, call or send a card, and send flowers. Tears are okay, but not too many. If you start to fall apart, get yourself together. Fall apart alone.

What is helpful…

- It normalized death for me. Going to a funeral home or being around a dead body does not freak me out. I learned how to initially reach out to people who are hurting

What I would change…

- There is no right or wrong way to grieve. It's okay to fall apart. It's okay to cry in front of other people. It's normal. You need support from others to get through hard things.

Session 3: Family Matters—How Our Attachents Affect Our Grief   39

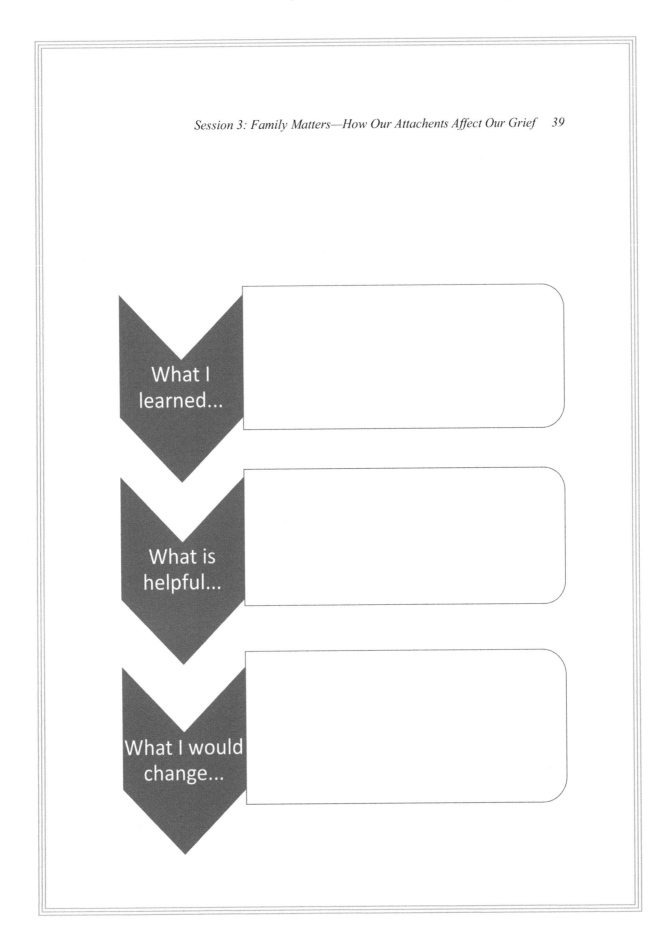

What I learned...

What is helpful...

What I would change...

Session 4: Identity: Who am I Now? Facilitator Review

Background Information

The obvious loss in death is the primary loss of the physical presence of the person who died. In the immediate aftermath of the death, we experience the heartbreak and overwhelming pain from the loss of our loved one's life. As time goes on the bereaved will experience other losses as a result of the death, called secondary losses. These may include financial losses, loss of a home and other material possessions, loss of structure, loss of goals, loss of hope, loss of faith/spiritual connection, and loss of identity (Williams, 2013).

People tend to identify themselves in response to what they do, who they are in relationship to others, and the environment in which they exist. People juggle multiple identities at once: child, parent, sibling, partner, friend, co-worker, manager, employee, and the list goes on. These identities help us form a sense of who we are in the world depending on the situations and the surrounding environments. Grief often makes us question our identity. Claire Phipps writes, "The loss of a loved one has a significant impact on one's sense of self due to the impact it has on the identities that comprise it" (2018, 464).

One of the responses to the death of a loved one is identity disturbance or "feeling as though part of oneself has died" (Harris, et al., 2021). Hernandez (2022) says, "We don't literally die, but our dreams for the person we hoped to be have died, and we must recognize that loss in order to move forward" (46). How we identify ourselves in relation to our loved ones impacts how we remember our loved ones, how we view ourselves now, and how we begin to move forward into a future without our loved ones physically present.

Research shows that developing a sense of self in the wake of the loss and grief is an important coping skill. Acknowledging the present reality, finding ways to remember and honor your loved one, and discovering who you are now are important parts of the grief process. Part of this task is to acknowledge the loss of the future you envisioned with your loved one and find ways to continue to make meaning in your life (Thomsen, et al., 2018). Personal transformation, healing, and growth can occur in the wake of grief, but the griever must be attentive to the experience for transformation to take place and offer themselves grace, patience, and compassion on this journey. (Phipps, 2018).

This session uses the story of Theseus' ship to talk about the question of identity. Legend says that Theseus, mythical Greek king of Athens rescued kidnapped children from an evil king and escaped on a ship. This legend was remembered in Athens each year by a pilgrimage in the same ship. Over time the ship was preserved by taking away the old planks as they decayed and putting in new, stronger timbers in their place. Theseus' Ship became a thought experiment for philosophers about whether or not an object whose original parts are entirely replaced over time remains the same object. One side argued the ship remained the same, and the other contended that it was not the same. After the parts are replaced, is it still Theseus' ship? (Wikipedia, n.d.)

The death of a loved one is often a before-and-after moment in which people often feel they are not the same person after the death of their loved one as they were before. Like Theseus' ship, we wonder after all this change, am I still who I was once or am I someone completely different. This session allows participants to explore who they have been, who they are now, and who they are becoming. When our loved one died, we may have lost hope in some parts of life. But hope is not a single entity; rather, it is "a collection of smaller hopes" (Pone, 2017, 112). Hope endures, but we have to learn to identify new hope for ourselves. Participants will be asked to redefine their hope for the future in the activity portion.

Session 4: Identity: Who am I Now?
From Page 41, Participant Guide

Goals

- Discuss how grief affects our sense of identity.

- Explore the importance of meaning-making in grief work.

Objectives

- Participants will identify ways their identity has changed as a result of their loss.

- Participants will identify areas of meaning in their lives and the life of their loved one.

Group Rules

Take a moment to review the group rules we established in the initial session.

These build psychological safety for our sessions.

1. Confidentiality: Group topics stay within group time. The facilitators are mandated reporters and will have to report any suicidal thoughts, homicidal thoughts/threats, and child elder abuse as part of our safety protocols. Beyond those issues, it is expected that both facilitators and participants maintain confidentiality about the things discussed in the group setting.

2. Respect: Do not interrupt or talk over each other. Do not engage in conversations while a topic is being discussed. Allow everyone an opportunity to speak.

3. Engagement: Active participation is expected during group sessions. The group develops and grows when everyone participates.

4. Communication: Speak from an "I" perspective. Do not assume to know what others are thinking and do not speak for anyone but yourself.

Mindfulness Exercise

Place both feet on the floor, hands in a comfortable position and sit up in order to facilitate deep breathing. Close your eyes or focus your gaze and take a couple of deep breaths to settle yourself. Notice how your body feels. Where are you holding any stress? Move those areas in a gentle way, stretching to find a sense of release. Open your mind to what is happening in your body and spirit and complete the statement:

- "I am aware of . . ." Maybe it's emptiness, loneliness, sadness, excitement or agitation.

- Where does this feeling reside in my body?

- How big is this feeling? What shape is it?

- What lies underneath this feeling: fear, shame, anger, longing?

Let go of any story that you are telling yourself and focus on the physical sensation that is happening right now. Place a hand where you are experiencing this sensation, sending comfort and peace to that part of the body. Begin to soften the area where the tension lies and let go of the difficult emotion that is causing the tension. Find a sense of release as you imagine letting go of the tension and difficult emotion with every exhale. Offer yourself compassion in this moment:

- May I be happy.

- May I know peace.

- May I be free from suffering.

Allow the compassion and peace to flow throughout your body. Bring your attention to your breath. Take a couple of deep breaths in and out. Feel the weight of your body in the chair, your feet on the floor, and pat your legs to bring your awareness back to the room. When you are ready, open your eyes and bring yourself back to the group. (adapted from Stang, H. 2021)

Check-in

Check in with the group about last week's homework and a brief overview of what participants have experienced since last group.

Psychoeducation

Legend says that Theseus, mythical Greek king of Athens, once rescued kidnapped children from an evil king and escaped on a ship. This legend was remembered in Athens each year by making a pilgrimage in the same ship. Theseus' ship was preserved by the Athenians over time by taking away the old planks as they decayed and putting in new, stronger timber in their places. The "Ship of Theseus" became a thought experiment for philosophers about whether or not an object whose original parts are entirely replaced over time remains the same object. One side argued the ship remained the same, while the other contended that it was not the same ship. (Ship of Theseus 2023)

Like Theseus' ship, grief makes us question our identity. One of the responses to the death of a loved one is identity disruption, a "feeling as though part of oneself has died" (Harris, et al., 2021). Hernandez (2022) says, "We don't literally die, but our dreams for the person we hoped to be have died, and we must recognize that loss in order to move forward" (46). We tend to identify ourselves in response to what we do, who we are in relationship to others, and our environment. We juggle multiple identities at once: child, parent, sibling, partner, friend, co-worker, manager, employee, and the list goes on. These identities help us form a sense of who we are in the world, depending on the situations and environments around us. Claire Phipps writes, "The loss of a loved one has a significant impact on one's sense of self due to the impact it has on the identities that comprise it" (2018, 464). How we identify ourselves in relation to our loved ones impacts how we remember our loved ones, how we view ourselves now, and how we begin to move forward into a future without our loved ones physically present.

Process Question

- How has your sense of self/identity changed since the death of your loved one?

- How has the loss changed you?

- What do you miss the most about your life before this loss?

Research shows that developing a sense of self in the wake of the loss and grief is an important coping skill. Acknowledging the present reality, finding ways to remember and honor your loved one, and discovering who you are now are important parts of the grief process. Part of this task is to acknowledge the loss of the future you envisioned with your loved one and find ways to continue to make meaning in your life (Thomsen, et al., 2018). Personal transformation, healing, and growth can occur in the wake of grief, but the griever must be attentive to the experience for this transformation to take place and to offer themselves grace, patience, and compassion on this journey. (Phipps, 2018).

Process Question

- How has your dream of the future changed because of your loss?

- Who are you becoming and how are you treating this new version of yourself?

- Do you like yourself right now?

Activity

One way we look forward to the future is by redefining hope. When our loved one died, we may have lost hope in some parts of life. But hope is not a single entity, rather, it is "a collection of smaller hopes" (Pone, 2017, 112). Hope endures, but we have to learn to identify new hope for ourselves. In the wake of her daughter's death, Lucy Pone (2017) writes, "I redefined hope by first selecting a more realistic goal: 'I hope that tomorrow I find the strength to endure whatever I have to face.' Then I clearly defined multiple pathways to reach my new goal: 'If something bad happens again, I will lean on my friends and family for strength.' My sense of agency came from remembering what I had already managed to endure and appreciating my strengthened resilience" (177).

She offers the following questions to help identify new hope for yourself in the face of loss:

- What has given you hope in the past?

- What things matter most to you now?

- What are you hoping for in this moment?

- What can you do to get closer to your hopes or goals?

Homework

- Write your next chapter: What gives your life meaning right now? What do you look forward to? What are you learning about yourself in your grief process? What are your hopes for the future?

- Honoring your loved one: Be prepared to share a story about your loved one next week. It can be a funny story, a happy memory, or something about who they were. Bring a picture to share with the group.

Session 5: Trauma and Grief Facilitator Review

Background Information

Traumatic grief occurs as the result of a sudden, unexpected loss. Traumatic grief refers to death as the result of an accident, murder, suicide, sudden health event, or "out-of-order deaths" such as the death of a child (Wolfelt, 2014, 54). Based on the suddenness, violence, and sense of justice associated with the loss, an individual may suffer trauma and grief simultaneously (Regehr & Sussman, 2004). Gamino, et al. states, "The unexpectedness of such deaths may hit like a body blow that throws survivors off balance and leaves them staggering to regain their emotional footing. That 'out of the blue' or 'I never saw it coming' quality can be very unsettling. Survivors left without any opportunity for leave taking or having the chance to say goodbye are at higher risk for grief-related distress" (2021, 341).

While most people manage this type of grief without seeking professional help, for many this type of loss can lead to post traumatic stress, major depressive disorder and "persistent, distressing, and disabling grief" (Boelen, et al., 2019, 2). MDD and PTSD are present in 10%-20% and 12%-27% respectively of bereaved individuals (Waller, et al., 2016, 133). After a traumatic death such as a suicide or homicide, many people describe a "don't ask, don't tell" attitude towards the experience (Clements, et al., 2004, 149). Deaths that leave the deceased's body burned or disfigured in some way often leave the survivors imagining the images of their loved one's final moments. If the body of the deceased is not able to be viewed, survivors are left without "clear evidence of the death that seeing the deceased's body provides" (Gamino, et al., 2021 341).

Individuals experiencing traumatic grief are at risk of developing complex grief reactions (Cowdrey & Stirling, 2020). Other life stressors such as physical and mental health challenges, financial struggles, and other life events can make grief complicated as well (Wolfelt, 20214, 58). Grief may trigger trauma responses invoked when we believe we are in danger. These responses may be experienced in our body as physical responses, behavioral changes, and emotional responses (Regehr & Sussman, 2004). If the person grieving already has PTSD from a separate traumatic event, grief from a new event could trigger PTSD symptoms. Tolstikova et al. (2005) state these reactions may be characterized as "fear, helplessness, and horror. . . increased arousal, difficulty falling or staying asleep, difficulty concentrating, hypervigilance, and outbursts of anger" (294). A common response to the discomfort of trauma responses is the desire to avoid or ignore the pain; however, avoidance does not take the trauma or pain away (Clements et al., 2004, 149). Wolfelt (2014) states that many people "fear that their pain will be limitless;" however, opening up to the pain is "necessary in the healing process" (114).

The recent traumatic losses during the COVID-19 pandemic coupled with the disrupted death rituals has made bereavement care a public health concern. Research shows prolonged, unattended grief and the loneliness that ensues creates adverse mental, emotional, and physical health problems (Cacciatore, et al., 2021). Evidence-based interventions which reduce the burden of suffering can reduce long-term health risks. (Waller, et al., 2016). Recent studies have shown that grieving people desire space to share their grief experience with others who can listen without trying to fix them or judge them. Studies show that spending time with others who share a common grief experience was helpful, whether it was in person or online, especially when the grief is traumatic (Cacciatore, et al., 2021).

Researchers suggest addressing meaning-making, using self-compassion for emotional distress, and dealing with shame and guilt are vital in addressing traumatic loss. Research suggests that interventions for complicated grief should focus on the attachment between the griever and their deceased loved one to help the bereaved adjust to life without their loved one (Supiano and Luptak, 2013). It is important to note that finding meaning is not the same as finding the reason that something happened. Everything does not have to happen for a reason. Megan Devine says, "To live a life of meaning is to find your own internal compass and to follow it as you honor your commitments to yourself, to others, and to the world (2021, 181). "Reevaluating our life in response to trauma doesn't necessarily mean changing every part of our life. . . The key is to ask the questions and to remain open to new answers. This is how we build the life that fits our new selves best." (Hernandez, 2022, 74).

Session 5: Trauma and Grief

From Page 47, Participant Guide

Goals

- Explore issues related to experiencing a sudden death of a loved one.

- Discuss how their current grief is impacted by past loss or trauma.

Objectives

- Participants will learn how trauma affects the grief process.

- Participants will identify where they are finding meaning and how they honor the memory of their loved one.

Group Rules

Take a moment to review the group rules we established in the initial session. These build psychological safety for our sessions.

1. Confidentiality: Group topics stay within group time. The facilitators are mandated reporters and will have to report any suicidal thoughts, homicidal thoughts/threats, and child elder abuse as part of our safety protocols. Beyond those issues, it is expected that both facilitators and participants maintain confidentiality about the things discussed in the group setting.

2. Respect: Do not interrupt or talk over each other. Do not engage in conversations while a topic is being discussed. Allow everyone an opportunity to speak.

3. Engagement: Active participation is expected during group sessions. The group develops and grows when everyone participates.

4. Communication: Speak from an "I" perspective. Do not assume to know what others are thinking and do not speak for anyone but yourself.

Mindfulness Exercise

To begin, place your feet flat on the floor, place your hands in a comfortable position, sit up so that you are not slouching, and either close your eyes or find a place to focus your gaze. Think about a place you consider a safe space. This could be somewhere in your home, outside, or even somewhere from your past.

- Imagine what you would see there. What does it look like? Are you inside or outside? Do you see plants, animals, other people? Is it bright or is the light low?

- Now, imagine what you would hear there. Are there nature sounds like waves or a crackling fire? Is the wind blowing? Is there music and laughter or conversation? Or is it quiet?

- What does it feel like there? Is it hot, cold, or just right? Do you need a blanket or are you enjoying a breeze on a summer day? Can you feel the sun on your face, the splash of water on your toes, the warmth by a fire, or the soft cushion of your favorite chair?

- What can you touch there? Are there rocks or shells you can pick up? Is there a soft, furry pet with you or maybe a fluffy pillow? Can you reach out and touch the bark of trees, the cool water, the sand, or the floor beside you?

- What can you smell or eat there? Is your favorite food cooking? Do you smell the salt in the air, the scent of pine, the burning wood from the fire, or the hot cocoa?

Take one last look around at your safe space. Take a couple of deep breaths and let yourself enjoy the beauty. Feel the weight of your body in the chair, your feet on the floor, your hands on your lap, and when you're ready you can open your eyes. Share with the group where you were and what that experience was like.

Check-in

Check in with the group about last week's homework. Participants were asked to be prepared to share a story about their loved one. It can be a funny story, a happy memory, or something about who they were. They might also bring a picture to share with the group.

Psychoeducation

Traumatic grief occurs as the result of a sudden, unexpected loss. Traumatic grief refers to death as the result of an accident, murder, suicide, sudden health event, or "out-of-order deaths" such as the death of a child (Wolfelt, 2014, 54). Based on the suddenness, violence, and sense of injustice associated with the loss, an individual may suffer trauma and grief simultaneously (Regehr & Sussman, 2004). While grief is the experience of reacting to the loss of a loved one, traumatic grief acknowledges the traumatic event as well as the grief process (Wolfelt, 2014, 34). After a traumatic death such as a suicide or homicide, many people describe a "don't ask, don't tell" attitude towards the experience (Clements, et al., 2004, 149). Individuals experiencing traumatic grief are at risk of developing complex grief reactions (Cowdrey & Stirling, 2020). Other life stressors such as physical and mental health challenges, financial struggles, or other life events can make grief complicated as well (Wolfelt, 20214, 58).

Grief may trigger trauma responses invoked when we believe we are in danger. These responses may be experienced in our body as physical responses, as behavioral changes, or as emotional responses (Regehr & Sussman, 2004). If the person grieving already has PTSD from a separate traumatic event, grief from a new event could trigger PTSD symptoms. Tolstikova et al. (2005) state these reactions may be characterized as "fear, helplessness, and horror. . . increased arousal, difficulty falling or staying asleep, difficulty concentrating, hyper-vigilance, and outbursts of anger (294). A common reaction to the discomfort of trauma responses is the desire to avoid or ignore the pain. However, avoidance does not take away the trauma or the pain (Clements et al., 2004, 149). Wolfelt (2014) states that many people "fear that their pain will be limitless." Instead, however, opening up to the pain is "necessary in the healing process" (114).

While grief can shatter one's assumptions about the world and disrupt one's belief system, unexpressed grief "destroys people's enthusiasm for life and living" (Wolfelt, 2014, 101). Healing requires integration to process the trauma, to discover how our past, present, and future are interconnected, and to understand how they influence our lives (Hernandez, 2022, 5). Integration is the concept of blending our experiences from the past, present, and future into the whole of who we are. Hernandez (2022) states, "We need to understand our past to make sense of our reactions, fears, and even strengths in the present" (4). To build resilient traits it is important to reconstruct meaning by integrating the loss into your life and finding ways to reconnect to self, to others, to the world, and to one's spirituality. (Zhai and Du, 2020)

Process Question

Michelle Hernandez in *Different After You: Rediscovering Yourself and Healing After Grief and Trauma* (2022) writes, "In the immediate aftermath of a traumatic experience, triage is usually the first step. To assign degrees of urgency to our needs and to deal with them in the order of critical importance requires focused energy" (1).

- What trauma responses are you noticing in yourself?
- What assumptions/beliefs have been shattered by your loss?
- What is helping you manage the pain?

Activity

Finding meaning in life is an important part of the healing process. Finding meaning is not the same as finding the reason that something happened. Megan Devine says, "To live a life of meaning is to find your own internal compass and to follow it as you honor your commitments to yourself, to others, and to the world (2021, 181). "Reevaluating our life in response to trauma doesn't necessarily mean changing every part of our life. The key is to ask the questions and to remain open to new answers. This is how we build the life that fits our new selves best." (Hernandez, 2022, 74).

- Identify and share with the group a meaningful moment from your life with your loved one.
- Describe the legacy of your loved one. What was important to them? How can you honor their them in your life and the world around you?

- What has been meaningful to you since your loved one died? Has there been a time you experienced his or her presence, when someone said or did something meaningful, or when you found meaning in something that happened?

Homework

Take some time to journal using one of the following starters:

- My biggest struggle right now is....

- I feel lonely when....

- I stay connected with my loved one by....

- One of the things I am learning right now is....

Session 6: Spirituality and Grief Facilitator Review

Background Information

Spirituality is foundational to every person's life. Lövgren et al. (2019) states, "Religion includes congregational aspects and formal ways to express one's beliefs, whereas spirituality is about personal authenticity, for example connecting with oneself, nature, or God/life sources. An individual may be spiritual without having a specific religion or very religious without having a developed spirituality." Spirituality can be seen "as a journey towards discovering and realizing one's fundamental aspirations" that explore the interconnectedness of life (Medhipour et al., 2020). They write, "Spiritual-religious practices and beliefs such as prayer, meditation, and engaging in enjoyable spiritual activities lead people away from their empty lives, suffering, and pain and causes one to tend toward creative and valuable activities" (17).

Our spiritual and religious beliefs are also a significant link to cultural traditions which often provide "a foundation and a context of meaning for death" (Ellis & Garske, 2007). Many Western religions espouse a belief in an afterlife where judgment regarding one's life choices and actions takes place. Eastern religions focus more on the cycle of life and may teach reincarnation of souls. No matter the belief, it is important to explore how spiritual practices may support and/or complicate the grief process (Doka and Chow, 2021, 245). Some individuals may feel their worldview has shattered in the grief process making it difficult to reconstruct meaning. Others may experience feeling the presence of their loved one with them or receive messages from their loved ones in manifestations in nature or in dreams (2021, 240-241). These moments of connection can bring great comfort to the bereaved and for some affirm religious beliefs about the afterlife (Schacter, et al., 2021, 327). These experiences also represent the continuing bonds theory that posits continuing the relationship with the deceased provides support for adjustment during the grief process

Meaningful bonds may be nurtured through talking to the deceased, thinking about them, keeping belongings of the deceased, or visiting places that were special to the deceased (2021, 321).

Multiple studies show that spiritual and religious connections can be a source of resilience, hope and post-traumatic growth in the grief process through the following ways:

- Use of rituals to memorialize the deceased

- Connection to Higher Power providing a sense of safety and comfort

- Connection to community reminding us we are not alone in the world

- Normalization of suffering in the world

- Continuing bonds with the deceased to provide continuity of living

- Belief in an afterlife with promise that we will see them again

- Meaning-making and religious coping help create purpose for the bereaved

- Spiritual practices such as prayer/meditation help regulate emotion

- Spiritual/religious symbols representing the departed individual may be of therapeutic value

- Use of gratitude practice created a more hopeful outlook

- Understanding the circle of life in nature helps with acceptance of death as a normal part of life

Complicated spiritual grief occurs when the bereaved experiences a spiritual crisis that compromises the person's relationship with God/Higher Power (Zampitella et al., 2023). Negative religious coping may result in feelings of being cut-off from spiritual/religious beliefs and can lead to complicated grief (Juekstock, 2018). This disconnection can be the result of blame/anger toward Higher Power, perceived punishment, or feeling abandoned by a Higher Power or community. These negative forms of religious coping may lead to emotional dysregulation and prolonged intensity of grief reactions (Lee et al, 2021). Violent deaths often lead to complicated grief and spiritual crisis leading to disruption in the bereaved's spiritual practice and challenges to their beliefs. One study reported bereaved individuals felt betrayed and abandoned by the negative response or lack-of response by their community of faith. The disconnection from the spiritual community led to feelings of abandonment by Higher Power (Godin, 2017).

Spiritual bypassing is a term coined by psychotherapist John Wellwood in the 1980's to describe "spiritual ideas and practices to sidestep personal, emotional 'unfinished business', to shore up a shaky sense of self, or to belittle basic needs, feelings and developmental tasks" (Soni, 2020). Spiritual bypassing "is the use of spiritual practices and beliefs to avoid dealing with our painful feelings, unresolved wounds, and developmental needs" (Masters, 2010, 1). Any belief, mantra, catchphrase, or misused sacred text that is used to distance us from our pain with superficial sayings or toxic positivity falls into this category. It is something we have all done and sometimes others do to us. Anytime we try to avoid or numb our pain because we "should" or "should not" feel a certain way, we are bypassing our pain. Anytime someone else shuts down your pain with a cliché because they are uncomfortable, they are bypassing your pain. "Cutting through spiritual bypassing means turning toward the painful, disfigured, ostracized, unwanted, or otherwise disowned aspects of ourselves and cultivating as much intimacy as possible with them" (Masters, 2010, 13). The key is to recognize the avoidance, normalize your difficult emotions, reconnect with the hope and meaning from your spirituality, be gentle and loving with yourself, and find someone who can help hold your pain.

Signs of spiritual bypassing include avoiding anger and other uncomfortable emotions, toxic positivity (looking for the positive in every situation), and denial of reality. It sounds like:

- Everything happens for a reason
- It was a blessing in disguise.
- It's all for the best.
- God's got a plan.
- Good vibes only!
- What doesn't kill you makes you stronger.

Using spiritual bypassing long term can lead to anxiety, shame, confusion, codependency, and depression. To begin healing, one must name and accept their emotions as part of the grief experience. Avoidance leads to a longer grief journey (Soni, 2020).

It is essential to allow spiritual/religious questioning during this session. Hopefully you have created a safe space in which participants feel they can share their thoughts and emotions with each other. Allow space for your own discomfort. Doubt and faith go hand in hand. There are no answers to the "why" questions but asking them and knowing others are asking the same thing brings some relief. Do not try to answer the questions or feel the need to defend Higher Power. Make space for their pain and listen. We will always have questions when it comes to death and dying but having a safe space to name those questions with others who have walked a similar road allows for growth.

Session 6: Spirituality and Grief

From Page 51, Participant Guide

Goals

- Discuss how spirituality can affect grief.
- Explore ways to connect with our personal spirituality.

Objectives

- Participants will identify ways their spiritual connections are helpful to them during the grief process.
- Participants will learn about spiritual bypassing and identify ways they may use their spirituality as a tool of avoidance.
- Participants will identify ways they can continue to connect to self, with others, with a Higher Power, or to nature, beauty, joy, and meaning in their daily lives.

Group Rules

Take a moment to review the group rules we established in the initial session. These build psychological safety for our sessions.

1. Confidentiality: Group topics stay within group time. The facilitators are mandated reporters and will have to report any suicidal thoughts, homicidal thoughts/threats, and child elder abuse as part of our safety protocols. Beyond those issues, it is expected that both facilitators and participants maintain confidentiality about the things discussed in the group setting.

2. Respect: Do not interrupt or talk over each other. Do not engage in conversations while a topic is being discussed. Allow everyone an opportunity to speak.

3. Engagement: Active participation is expected during group sessions. The group develops and grows when everyone participates.

4. Communication: Speak from an "I" perspective. Do not assume to know what others are thinking and do not speak for anyone but yourself.

Mindfulness Exercise

In his 2022 online article *Honoring Grief,* Jack Kornfield teaches how to meditate on grief. What follows is an excerpt from that article that we will use as our meditation for today:

> To meditate on grief, let yourself sit alone or with a comforting friend. Take the time to create an atmosphere of support. Sense a field of strength and support wherever you can, of your loved ones, of your spiritual teachers, of Mother Earth, [of God] who has seen it all. When you are ready, begin by tuning in to your breath. Feel your breathing in the area of your chest. This can help you become present to what is within you. Take one hand and hold it gently on your heart as if you were holding a vulnerable human being. You are.

> As you continue to breathe, bring to mind the loss or pain you are grieving. Let the story, the images, the feelings come naturally. Hold them gently. Take your time. Let the feelings come layer by layer, a little at a time.

> Keep breathing softly, compassionately. Let whatever feelings are there, pain and tears, anger and love, fear and sorrow, come as they will. Touch them gently. Let them unravel out of your body and mind. Make space for any images that arise. Allow the whole story. Breathe and hold it all with tenderness and compassion. Kindness for it all, for you and for others.

> The grief we carry is part of the grief of the world. Hold it gently. Let it be honored. You do not have to keep it in anymore. You can let it go into the heart of compassion; you can weep.

> Releasing the grief we carry can be a long, tear-filled process. Yet it follows the natural intelligence of the body and heart. Trust it, trust the unfolding. Along with meditation, some of your grief will want

to be written in pages or poems. Some will need to be cried out, to be sung, to be danced. Let the timeless wisdom within you carry you through grief and awaken a tender, open heart.

Keep in mind that grief doesn't just dissolve. You will notice how grief arises in waves and gradually, with growing compassion, there comes more space around it. Let it take its time. The heart opens in its own season, and little by little, gaps of new life—breaks in the rain clouds—appear. The body relaxes and freer breaths appear. This is a natural cycle you can trust: how life—and the heart—renews itself. Like the spring after winter, it always does.

Check-in

Check in with participants about the journaling homework..

Psychoeducation

Spirituality is foundational to every person's life. Löygren et al. (2019) states, "Religion includes congregational aspects and formal ways to express one's beliefs, whereas spirituality is about personal authenticity—for example, connecting with oneself, nature, or God/life sources. An individual may be spiritual without having a specific religion or very religious without having a developed spirituality." Spirituality can be seen "as a journey towards discovering and realizing one's fundamental aspirations" in a journey that explores the interconnectedness of life (Mehdipour et al., 2020). Our spiritual and religious beliefs are also a significant link to cultural traditions which often provide "a foundation and a context of meaning for death" (Ellis & Garske, 2007). Mehdipour et al. (2020) writes, "Spiritual-religious practices and beliefs such as prayer, meditation, and engaging in enjoyable spiritual activities lead people away from their empty lives, from

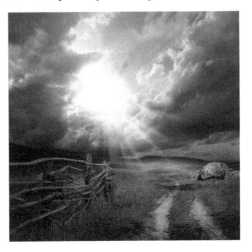

suffering, and from pain. These practices cause one to tend toward creative and valuable activities" (17). Multiple studies show that spiritual and religious connections can be a source of resilience, hope and post-traumatic growth in the grief process through the following ways:

- Using rituals to memorialize the deceased

- Connecting to a Higher Power to provide a sense of safety and comfort

- Connecting to the community to remind us we are not alone in the world

- Normalizing the suffering in the world to understand that we are not alone

- Continuing bonds with the deceased to provide continuity of living

- Believing in an afterlife to be comforted with the promise that we will see the person again

- Coping through meaning-making and religious faith to help create purpose for the bereaved

- Using spiritual practices such as prayer/meditation to help regulate emotions

- Using spiritual/religious symbols representing the departed individual to produce therapeutic value

- Using a practice of gratitude to create a more hopeful outlook

- Understanding nature's circle of life to help with acceptance of death as a normal part of life

Complicated spiritual grief occurs when the bereaved experiences a spiritual crisis that compromises the person's relationship with God/Higher Power (Zampitella et al., 2023). Negative religious coping may result in feelings of being cut-off from spiritual/religious beliefs, thus leading to complicated grief (Juekstock, 2018). This disconnection can be the result of blame/anger toward Higher Power caused by the perception of punishment or being abandoned by a Higher Power or by their faith community. These negative forms of religious coping may lead to emotional dysregulation and prolonged intensity of grief reactions (Lee et al, 2021). Violent deaths often lead to complicated grief and a spiritual crisis which leads to disruption in the bereaved's spiritual practice and to challenges to beliefs. One study reported bereaved individuals felt betrayed and abandoned by the negative response or lack-of response from their community of faith. The disconnection from the spiritual community led to feelings of abandonment by the Higher Power (Godin, 2017).

Spiritual bypassing "is the use of spiritual practices and beliefs to avoid dealing with our painful feelings, unresolved wounds, and developmental needs" (Masters, 2010, 1). Any belief, mantra, catchphrase, or misused sacred text that is used to distance us from our pain with superficial sayings or toxic positivity falls into this category. It is something we have all done and sometimes others have done to us. Anytime we try to avoid or numb our pain because we "should" or "should not" feel a certain way indicates that we are bypassing our pain. Anytime someone else shuts down our pain with a cliché because *they* are uncomfortable also creates a bypassing of our pain. "Cutting through spiritual bypassing means turning toward the painful, disfigured, ostracized, unwanted,

Spiritual Bypassing is actually the body's defense mechanism. It is about using spiritual ideas to run away from unresolved issues.

SPIRITUAL BYPASSING	VS	SPIRITUALITY

 Prohibits to express emotions

 Don't feel pain as they don't acknowledge it

 Experiences nervousness, anxiety attacks, stress

 Emphasizes to express emotions

 Acknowledges the pain & learn to control the emotions

 Calmness is the virtue of practicing spirituality

WAYS TO STOP SPIRITUAL BYPASSING

- Acknowledge your weakness
- Take feedback
- Face your emotions & pain
- Have a honest chat with yourself

or otherwise disowned aspects of ourselves and cultivating as much intimacy as possible with them" (Masters, 2010, 13). The key is to recognize the avoidance, normalizing our difficult emotions, and reconnecting with the hope and meaning from our spirituality. Be gentle and loving with ourselves, and find someone who can help hold our pain.

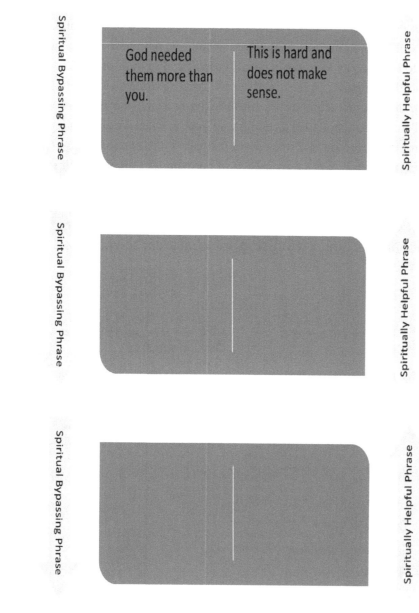

Process Questions

- What are some of the sayings you have said to yourself or heard from others that were meant to numb or avoid your pain?

- What would be helpful to hear instead?

- What spiritual beliefs or practices have been difficult for you in your grief?

- What spiritual beliefs, practices, or rituals help you cope with your grief?

Activity

Use the Spiritual Bypassing Rewrite sheet to explore some of the unhelpful spiritual bypassing phrases you have heard or said to yourself, then rewrite them to use as prayers or mantras in your spiritual practices.

Homework

Create a Loss Timeline that shows significant points of personal loss and transition throughout your life. Make note of your emotional, physical, spiritual, and practical responses to the losses. Use drawings, symbols, pictures to represent events. Make a list of previous coping strategies that helped you get through the loss.

Session 7: Expressing Grief—
Lament and Hope
Facilitator Review

Background Information

Fear, anger, anxiety, and meaninglessness are all normal feelings associated with grief. These are not "bad" emotions, as emotions are neither good nor bad, they just are. Dr. Alan Wolfelt (2014) states, "People in grief often blame themselves, others, and the world at large for their losses. They feel shame. They feel regret. They feel despair" (p.50). Difficult emotions are not to be ignored or overcome, rather they indicate pain and a need for comfort (Wolfelt, 2014, 51). Wolfelt writes, "When grief goes unexpressed, or unmourned, it destroys people's enthusiasm for life and living. . . The result is that these parts of themselves go stagnant or remain unclaimed inside of them" (2014, 101). Or as I like to say, "If you don't work on your grief, your grief will work on you!" When we ignore our pain, it tends to come out sideways at those people closest to us in agitation and angry outbursts or as withdrawal causing us to isolate ourselves from our loved ones.

Lament is one way to express that life is not right or as it is supposed to be. Lament is a form of writing that is a crying out of our pain and suffering. It is a form of release that occurs "when the dysfunction reaches an unacceptable level" (Bruggemann, 1995, 105). Life will always have stress and dysfunction, but we may experience a breaking point when the stress becomes more than we can handle. When that happens–and it will–you have to let it out. Lament can be found in operas, musicals, African American spirituals, blues, rock-n-roll, country music, poetry, and art—wherever grief is expressed, there is lament.

Lament deals with real life experiences in honest dialogue with God/Higher Power (Bruggemann, 1995). Ancient Israel used lament in their songbook- the Psalms. More than half of the songs are laments, either with the whole community or an individual crying out in pain and despair. This means half of the music in Israel's worship was dedicated to crying out, complaining, and even blaming God/Higher Power for the terrible situations of life. Imagine singing loudly, "My God, my God, why have you forsaken me?" (Psalm 22) or "You have put me in the lowest pit...darkness is my closest friend" (Psalm 88) as a part of your regular spiritual practice. Bill Bellinger writes,

"The psalms recognize even before modern psychology that we do not deal with pain by ignoring it but by acknowledging it and moving through it" (2012, 77).

Lamenting is not just about complaining. The true form of any lament ends with recalling the faithfulness of God/Higher Power and one's confidence in the hope for the future. Some even offer thanks for feeling a spiritual presence that provides solace in the midst of despair and suffering. Psalm 40 remembers the pain of the "pit" and the "mire" but asserts that Yahweh heard their cry of lament and rescued the psalmist. The psalmist has been set back on solid ground and been given a new song of praise. Kristin Swenson states in Living through Pain: Psalms and the Search for Wholeness, "The psalmist's declaration is a critical part of reclothing his soul, it gives to others who suffer affirmation of their humanity and worth, and it gives to the greater community powerful testimony of enduring goodness and grace" (2005, 174).

Lament is a way of surrendering to the idea that we cannot control our circumstances, but we can control how we handle ourselves in our suffering. Working through the pain helps give a sense of control and restores our connection to ourselves, others, and Higher Power (Beattie, 2006, 6). Bellinger writes, "The Psalms raise the issue of hope even in the face of pain, and hope can lead one through hardship and trial" (2012). We express our pain to relieve the stress of anger, disappointment, hurt, betrayal, resentment, and grief to make room for hope. Our hope is not that all the bad things will go away. Our hope is that when we feel our worst and are lonelier than we ever imagined we can find the power to keep moving forward (Bellinger, 2012).

Lament has a communal purpose. Lament reconnects us with people around the universal experience of pain and suffering. Even when we cannot be comforted in our misery, we are never alone. We find companionship on our journey from others who understand our pain, and from those who walk with us on this journey even when they don't know what to say or do for us. "Without faithful communal lament, private hurts live in tension with public joy. . . Without faithful communal lament, communities of faith do not share the hurt and pain of public, national or global tragedies and anxieties. Without faithful communal lament, we do not participate as communities in the realities of the human predicament. Consequently, we exist as superficial, inauthentic and uncaring communities in a fallen world filled with hurts and pains" (Hicks, 2005). Communal laments help the community move forward in the healing process. "It is only after we lament, after we face and express the pain and negativity and get it all out, that healing can begin. In more theological terms, we can say that it is only by facing and going through the death that we can come to new life, to resurrection" (Guinan, 2021).

Communal laments in the Hebrew Scripture express empathy for people suffering because of great loss or injustice. We empathize with those who are oppressed and are moved to action. God's people come together to petition God for help and to remember God's previous acts of love and salvation. Israel finds confidence to approach God in their distress because of their belief in God's everlasting faithfulness. Bruggemann states, "Indeed, it is the cry of Israel (Exodus 2.23-25) which mobilizes Yahweh to action that begins the history of Israel. The cry initiates history" (1986).

The form of lament helps us understand how Israel interpreted their pain from a context of faith. There is never an attempt to explain the hurt. For Israel, "understanding and experiencing are enough." The overall form of the lament focuses on transformation. There are typically five parts to any lament:

1. Address— describes who the lament is written to

2. Complaint—describes the situation/problem

3. Assurance of trust-expresses what you trust or have confidence in—your belief about what could happen

4. Petition—asks that the problem be dealt with

5. Gratitude/Praise—thanks for the transformation that is already taking place

During the group the facilitator will go through the questions to address each section of the lament. It is easiest to address the communal lament for this practice to "Grief" rather than God to be respectful of each participant's religious/spiritual preferences. As the participants address the questions of each part of the lament, the facilitator types their words verbatim. Ask them to repeat themselves, if necessary, but it is vital for the practice that the finished product is made up of their own words. An example from a former group is below. Each paragraph represents the different parts of the lament. This group chose to address the lament to important people in their life rather than to grief itself. The formatting is my personal choice.

February 2021 Grief Group Communal Lament

We cry out to our pastors, the Lord, our family members and friends,

 the people closest to us, our immediate family.

Every week, every time we turn around,

 there is someone passing away from this deadly virus.

We know that all life will come to an end,

 but it hurts that we are no longer able to be there for them.

We are no longer able to be there to hold them.

We are no longer able to say good-bye.

Why was my brother, our loved ones, taken away from us at this time?

Why did they leave so soon? It was all so unexpected.

Why did they have to leave the way they left? Why did it have to be so horrific?

A lot of this was avoidable. It didn't have to happen the way it did.

This could have been avoided, and I am angry and frustrated about it.

Why do we hurt so bad? We have never felt pain like we feel.

Our hearts hurt.

We are praying for peace, comfort, and strength.

We just want to try to find closure.

We want to come to terms with what happened.

What can we do to relieve the pressure and pain?

We need clarity. We need to understand what you are trying to teach us.

We want to get back to some type of normalcy.

We will never forget them, but how do we move on?

We know through time, time will heal all,

    because we have experienced that many times in our lifetimes.

We know that we will get through this, too.

We know that life will continue, and that we will have positive times and negative.

Without a doubt, we know my parents and loved ones are with their Maker—they are in a

    better place.

We believe we will see them again.

Our confidence is in God/our Maker, knowing that some things are out of our control,

    but God is in control.

There was nothing we could do to stop our loved ones from passing away.

We are thankful for the time we had with our loved ones.

We are thankful that every day we look in the mirror

    and look in the eyes looking back at us,

    we know our loved ones are still here.

Their spirit, and what they have given us in life lives on as long as we maintain.

We are very thankful for the outstanding support

    from family members and friends through the hard time

    and the good sense and feeling that we are never alone moving forward.

Thank you for helping us with the hardest part

    and for giving us the strength to see our loved ones through.

Session 7: Expressing Grief— Lament and Hope

From Page 57, Participant Guide

Goals

- Discuss ways we express the pain of grief.

- Identify unhealthy and healthy ways we manage difficult emotions.

- Discuss the meaning of lament.

- Create a communal lament.

Objectives

- Participants will identify difficult emotions and how they manage them.

- Participants will create a communal lament to give expression to their experience of grief.

Group Rules

Take a moment to review the group rules we established in the initial session. These build psychological safety for our sessions.

1. Confidentiality: Group topics stay within group time. The facilitators are mandated reporters and will have to report any suicidal thoughts, homicidal thoughts/threats, and child elder abuse as part of our safety protocols. Beyond those issues, it is expected that both facilitators and participants maintain confidentiality about the things discussed in the group setting.

2. Respect: Do not interrupt or talk over each other. Do not engage in conversations while a topic is being discussed. Allow everyone an opportunity to speak.

3. Engagement: Active participation is expected during group sessions. The group develops and grows when everyone participates.

4. Communication: Speak from an "I" perspective. Do not assume to know what others are thinking and do not speak for anyone but yourself.

Mindfulness Exercise

Let's begin by placing both feet on the floor, hands in your laps, sitting up to allow expansion through the belly, and either close your eyes if you feel safe, or focus your eyes downward. Take a couple of deep, cleansing breaths and on the exhale let out an audible sigh. Be as loud as you want. Make it a guttural release. Do this one more time. Now, let's add arm movements to increase the sense of release. Place your arms down by your side, palms up. As you inhale, reach out and grab your stress, pain, negativity, etc. and pull it toward your chest in a fist. On your exhale, move your arms out to the side, releasing the palms as though your are throwing that pain and stress outside your body. Repeat this action a couple of times. Take some calming breaths. Feel the weight of your body in the chair, feel your feet on the floor, pat your legs, and when you are ready, you can open your eyes and come back to the room.

Check-in

Check in with the group about last week's homework and a brief overview of what participants have experienced since last group.

Psychoeducation

Fear, anger, anxiety, and meaninglessness are all normal feelings associated with grief. These are not "bad" emotions, as emotions are neither good nor bad—they just are. Dr. Alan Wolfelt (2014) states, "People in grief often blame themselves, others, and the world at large for their losses. They feel shame. They feel regret. They feel despair" (p.50). Dark emotions are not to be ignored or overcome. Rather, they indicate pain and a need for comfort (Wolfelt, 2014, 51). We have to find a way to express these difficult emotions in order to work through them. "When grief goes unexpressed or unmourned, it destroys people's enthusiasm for life and living. . . The result is that these parts of themselves go stagnant or remain unclaimed inside of them" (Wolfelt, 2014, 101). Or, as I like to say, "If you don't work on your grief, your grief will work on you!" When we ignore our pain, it tends to come out sideways at those closest to us through expressions of agitation and angry outbursts or as withdrawal that causes us to isolate ourselves from our loved ones.

Lament is one way to express that life is not right or as it is supposed to be. Lament is a form of writing that is a crying out of our pain and suffering. It is a form of release that occurs "when the dysfunction reaches an unacceptable level" (Bruggemann, 1995, 105). Lament is found throughout poetry, music, and in art (as seen in The Scream by Edvard Munch, 1893). The Hebrew scriptures even use lament in their songbook—the Psalms. More than half of the songs are laments, either with the whole community or by an individual crying out in pain and despair. Bill Bellinger writes, "The psalms recognize even before modern psychology that we do not deal with pain by ignoring it, but by acknowledging it and moving through it" (2012, 77).

Lament is a way of surrendering to the idea that we cannot control our circumstances, but we can control how we handle ourselves in our suffering. Working through the pain helps give a sense of control and restores our connection to ourselves, to others, and to a Higher Power (Beattie, 2006, 6). We express our pain to relieve the anger, disappointment, hurt, betrayal, and resentment in order to make room for hope. Our hope is that when we feel our worst and are lonelier than we ever imagined, we can find the power to keep moving forward (Bellinger, 2012).

Lament has a communal purpose. Lament reconnects us with people around the universal experience of pain and suffering. Even when we cannot be comforted in our misery, we are never alone. We find companionship on our journey from others who understand pain. We are with those who love us even when they don't know what to say or do for us, but who can walk with us on this journey. "Without faithful communal lament, we do not participate as communities in the realities of the human predicament. Consequently, we exist as superficial, inauthentic and uncaring communities in a fallen world filled with hurts and pains" (Hicks, 2018). "It is only after we lament, after we face and express the pain and negativity and get it all out, that healing can begin" (Guinan, 2018)

Activity

Psalm 88 is an example of a lament. As you read it notice how the writer expresses their pain and suffering. Most laments use phrases like, "How long?" and "Why?" and "When?" and end with some word of hope or praise. Note that this psalm one does not end that way, because some days there is no space for praise. What do you hear in this lament?

A Prayer When You Can't Find the Way (Psalm 88)

1   You keep me safe, LORD God.
       So when I pray at night,
2   please listen carefully to each of my concerns.
3   I am deeply troubled and close to death;
4   I am as good as dead and completely helpless.
5   I am no better off than those in the grave,
       those you have forgotten and no longer help.
6   You have put me in the deepest and darkest grave;
7   your anger rolls over me like ocean waves.
8   You have made my friends turn in horror from me.
    I am a prisoner who cannot escape,
9   and I am almost blind because of my sorrow.
    Each day I lift my hands in prayer to you, LORD.
10   Do you work miracles for the dead?
    Do they stand up and praise you?

11   Are your love and loyalty announced in the world of the dead?

12   Do they know of your miracles
>   or your saving power in the dark world below
>   where all is forgotten?

13   Each morning I pray to you, LORD.

14   Why do you reject me?
>   Why do you turn from me?

15   Ever since I was a child, I have been sick and close to death.
>   You have terrified me and made me helpless.

16   Your anger is like a flood!
>   And I am shattered by your furious attacks

17   that strike each day and from every side.

18   My friends and neighbors have turned against me because of you,
>   and now darkness is my only companion.

Next, we are going to work together to create our own group lament. We will address our lament to Grief itself. Your facilitator will type while you share what you feel when your facilitator asks these questions. After completing the lament, the facilitator will read it back to you.

Process Questions for Communal Lament

- What is your complaint to grief? What would you want to say about your grief experience? Remember that you can use the questions of "How long? Why? When?" to get you started.

- What do you want to happen right now? What would you ask for?

- Reality check: What do you know to be true right now? In what do you trust/have confidence?

- What are you grateful for in this moment?

- After hearing your communal lament, how does it feel to hear what you wrote together?

Meditation

Grieving is hard work, so before we go, we are going to take a moment to offer ourselves some kindness and compassion.

Self-Compassion Break

To practice self-compassion, we need to call up a little suffering. This could be some type of stress, a relationship problem, an uncertainty about your future, or feelings from the lament that you just wrote about—anything that is difficult for you right now, but not overwhelming.

Bring it to mind by thinking about: What is going on right now? What has happened? What might happen? Name the situation to get in touch with it. Then say these compassionate statements to yourself:

Three Compassionate Statements:

1. Bring to mind the fact that suffering is present. Use your own language that speaks to you.

- This is a moment of suffering.
- This is really hard.
- I'm really struggling.
- This sucks.

2. Remind yourself of our common humanity.

- Struggling is a part of life.
- It's normal to feel this way.

- I'm not alone in my suffering. Other people are suffering, too.

- Suffering is part of being a human being.

3. Show yourself some kindness in your suffering. Use language you would use with a good friend. Use a term of endearment if it feels good to you. Put your hands on your heart, head, belly—whatever feels comforting—and say the following to yourself.

- May I be at peace.

- It's going to be okay.

- You are cared for and loved.

- This is hard, sweetheart, but you can do this hard thing.

Now, allow yourself to be still and quiet, just as you are in this moment. Continue your deep breaths. Bring yourself back to this space. When you're bring your mind back to the room and open your eyes (Neff, n.d.).

Individual Lament

Psalms of lament remember better times and wish to return to those times. Lament gives expression to the real, sometimes painful, experiences of life. The purpose of lament is to express that life is not right—not as it was supposed to be. Lament is a way to cry out in hopes of getting help and changing your circumstances. Walter Bruggemann says, "Lament occurs when the dysfunction reaches an unacceptable level." (*Psalms and the Life of Faith*, p.105)

1. Address (Dear...)

2. Complaint (The real problem):

3. Request (What do you want to happen):

4. Expression of trust confidence (What you know is true):

5. Vow of praise/thanksgiving:

Homework

- Find someone with whom to share this lament with this week. If you want to write your own lament, use the process questions above as your guide.

- Melody Beattie writes in The Grief Club, ". . . we need to tell our story again even if we've already told it one hundred times before. It makes the unthinkable real. It gives us a sense of control. Telling our story is important." Research tells us that if you can write about your deepest emotions and thoughts regarding your grief (or any traumatic upheaval) for 20 minutes a day, 4 days in a row, it can decrease the intensity of the trauma. (Pennebaker, 2004, 26) Try the following Writing to Heal assignment this week.

If the above assignment is too difficult, consider simply answering the following questions:

- What is challenging me most right now?

- What went well today?

- How can I help show myself compassion today?

Writing to Heal

Research by J. Pennebaker (2004) in the aftereffects of trauma showed:

- People who have a traumatic experience and keep it secret are at higher risk for both major and minor illnesses.

This week set a time each day for at least four days in a row to write, following the guidelines below. You will not be asked to share what you write—rather about the experience of writing.

What to Write:

- Flip-Out Rule: If you feel you might get too upset while writing about a particular topic, don't write about it. If you think something will cause you to flip-out, write about something else.

- Start with an emotional upheaval that is bothering you. What has been keeping you awake at night?

- Trust where your writing takes you. If you begin writing about something else, go with it.

- Let sleeping dogs lie. Don't dredge up old issues that aren't relevant to you right now.

- Write only about traumas and upheavals of which you are aware, not repressed memories.

When & Where to Write:

- If possible, write at the same time every day to establish a writing ritual.

- If possible, find some "down time" when you can write.

- Studies show people have more success writing at the end of their workday. Most importantly is for you to have some free time to let you mind reflect on what you have written.

- Find a healing environment to do your writing. This can be a place that already exists for you or one you create yourself. It should be a place that provides you a sense of comfort.

66   From Loss to Life and Back Again

Writing Style:

- Your writing is private and for you alone.

- Acknowledge your emotions openly.

- Construct a coherent story.

- Find your voice.

- Don't overanalyze. If you feel you are not making progress, rethink your writing strategy.

- Try to write for 20 minutes a day without stopping.

Effects of Emotional Writing:

- General enhances immune function

- Produces better lung function among asthma patients

- Lowers pain and disease severity among arthritis sufferers

- Reduces immediate signs of stress

- Creates often a feeling of being sad/weepy in the short term, but creates a feeling of being happier and less negative in the long-term

- Boosts ability to think about/focus on complex tasks

- Increases social comfort and the ability to talk and laugh more with others, to listen better and to generally be more positive in social settings

- Alleviates anger

- Switches the perspective of your story—view it through others' eyes

Session 8: Resilience and Meaning-Making Facilitator Review

Background Information

Recent research by George Bonnano states over time, most people display natural resilience in coping with their grief effectively experiencing mild to moderate distress and returning to their baseline in 18 to 24 months (Milman, et al., 2021, 442). According to Bonnano, our grief reactions are "designed to help us accept and accommodate losses, usually relatively quickly, so that we can continue to live productive lives" (2019, 9). Bonnano found that only 10-15% of people suffer from chronic grief that can last for years and become disabling (2019, 8). Milman, et al., state this type of grief is a predictor of mental and physical health problems such as cardiovascular issues, cancer, depression, anxiety, and suicidality (2021, 442). Levels of distress increase to 30-70% when grieving a violent death such as a suicide, homicide, or fatal accident (Milman, et al., 2021, 448). Research from Prigerson, et al., has shown that "persistent intense grief symptoms may, indeed be pathological" and require targeted interventions (2021, 122).

Lucy Hone's book *Resilient Grieving: How to Find Your Way Through a Devastating Loss* offers a formula for building resilience in the grief process. Hone is a resilience researcher who in 2017 experienced the death of her 12-year-old daughter in a car accident in which Lucy's best friend and her best friend's daughter were also killed. She applied her resilience research to her own experience of grief and identified strategies that helped her manage her grief and find meaning in her life again. Hone recommends taking your time to be with the deceased and care for the body. She states you must allow yourself to feel the pain of the loss while still maintaining routines to create a sense of psychological safety. She encourages grievers to create rituals to mark the loss and honor the deceased. To foster ongoing resilience, she offers three strategies: understand that suffering is a part of life, make careful choices about where to focus your attention, and ask yourself, "Is what I'm doing right now helping me or harming me?" (Hone, 2017, 230).

Tedeschi and Calhoun's framework for post traumatic growth after traumatic events includes experiencing: a) a changed sense of self, feeling stronger/more independent, b) changes in interpersonal relationships to value intimacy and empathy, and c) spiritual/existential changes focusing on the present moment and gratitude (Gamino, et al., 2021 354). Neimeyer uses the process of meaning making and meaning reconstruction as a way for the bereaved to work through the loss. Neimeyer uses life narratives, benefit finding, and exploration of changes in the bereaved' s identity to help make sense of the loss. An example of benefit finding would be family relationships mended or a deeper gratitude for life because of the loss (Gilbet and Macpherson, 2021, 292). Benefit finding is not about finding a reason the person had to die for something good to happen. I do not condone the fallacy, "Everything happens for a reason" as this is often used as spiritual bypassing as discussed in the Spirituality and Grief session. I do believe there is always something to be grateful for in the moment and meaning can be found in our lives and in the legacies of our loved ones.

Survivors of traumatic losses may create meaning through working with victims' rights groups, seeking justice, honoring their loved one's life through volunteer work, starting a foundation, or supporting others in similar situations. Recent research shows that survivors who struggle with meaning making may experience more severe grief reactions long-term including post-traumatic stress (Bordere, et al., 2021, 399). Meaning making is an ongoing process. Some group members may feel it is too soon to do this work. Acknowledge their feelings and encourage them to share their experiences. Do not argue or try to convince them of the benefits of meaning making. Sharing their story is a way of making meaning in and of itself.

Session 8: Resilience and Meaning-Making

From Page 67, Participant Guide

Goals

- Explore ways to build resilience during grief.

Objectives

- Participants will identify existing areas of strength and resilience.
- Participants will identify potential coping strategies to help build resilience.

Group Rules

Take a moment to review the group rules we established in the initial session. These build psychological safety for our sessions.

1. Confidentiality: Group topics stay within group time. The facilitators are mandated reporters and will have to report any suicidal thoughts, homicidal thoughts/threats, and child elder abuse as part of our safety protocols. Beyond those issues, it is expected that both facilitators and participants maintain confidentiality about the things discussed in the group setting.

2. Respect: Do not interrupt or talk over each other. Do not engage in conversations while a topic is being discussed. Allow everyone an opportunity to speak.

3. Engagement: Active participation is expected during group sessions. The group develops and grows when everyone participates.

4. Communication: Speak from an "I" perspective. Do not assume to know what others are thinking and do not speak for anyone but yourself.

Mindfulness Exercise

Find a comfortable position with both feet on the floor, your arms resting comfortably, and sitting up to allow for a full breath. Today we are going to learn tactical breathing. This is a process where the exhale lasts longer than the inhale to enhance relaxation. Instructions are below, but feel free to adjust the count so that it is comfortable for you (Meichenbaum, 2012, 94-95).

The steps are:

- Breathe in through your nose for 6 counts

- Hold for two counts

- Breathe out through your mouth for ten counts as though blowing through a straw

- Hold for two counts

- Repeat this practice a few times

Check-in

- Did you find someone with whom to share this lament this week?

- Which writing assisgnment did you choose and what was your experience of completing the writing?

Activity

A regular practice of gratitude helps build resilience. Name a good thing that has happened today. What was the role you played in that good thing? (Pone, 2017)

Psychoeducation

Resilience is the ability to adapt to adversity and continue moving forward. Every life stressor challenges us in different ways. "The people who deal best with these different situations are those who can do what it takes to get through the event. . . It's a matter of doing what I can to get through each hour, day, week, month, and year" (Pone, 2017, 38-39). Resilient people differentiate between what they can and cannot change and focus on what is in their control. Resilient people problem-solve by identifying the old habits, thoughts, and behaviors that no longer serve them, and think flexibly and creatively to find the best way forward. (Pone, 2017, 108-110).

Sharing the impact of the loss, using rituals to mark the passing, adapting to new family structures, and finding resources to reduce the stress of the loss are vital strategies in building resilience (Özcan and Kaya, 2019). The griever makes choices about their healing process and they will not be forced to face something they are not ready to face in order to create a sense of safety. "Reliving painful feelings and taking risks are part of the healing process. But you are able to ask yourself, 'Is this the right time? Am I willing to go through this now?'" (Wolfelt, 2014, 115)

A willingness to consider new perspectives can help build resilience (Schwartz et al., 2018). "Being conscious that the present might be bad, but to keep looking forward to the future" is realistic optimism practiced by resilient people (Pone, 2017, 108). "Surprising realizations related to our experience, people who have come into our life during our healing, and dreams that we were afraid to express before may all become of primary importance in the new world we are building" (Hernandez, 2022, 73).

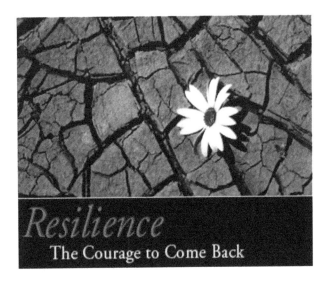

Process Questions

- What habits, thoughts, or behaviors no longer serve you in your grief? How are you changing them as you heal?

- Think about a time when you got through a difficult situation. What helped you get through that situation?

- What helps relieve the painful part of the healing process?

- Who are models of resilience in your life? How do they live out their resiliences?

Activity

One difficult work of grief is finding a way to incorporate the reality of the death into our world view. Our brain tries desperately to make sense of the loss to rewrite our life story as we adapt to the grief (Hone, 2017). Lucy Hone (2017) writes, "This kind of reframing is our brain's natural way of helping us cope. It involves shifting our perspective, choosing what we focus on" (179).

Hone (2017) quotes another grieving mom who stated, "Even in the darkest moments there were blessings. I had to choose to notice they were there" (178). This is not the same thing as trying to make sense of our loved one's death. Rather, this is finding meaning and areas of gratitude in your life now. Sheryl Sandberg, COO of Facebook, posted after her husband's sudden death in 2015 that she chooses life and meaning after her loss, "sharing what I have learned in the hope that it helps someone else, in the hope that there can be some meaning from this tragedy" (Pone, 2017, 182).

- How are you incorporating meaning into your life after your loss?

- Where are you finding hope?

Group Reflection

- What moments that stand to you throughout this group experience? What has been helpful?

Homework

- Create a written statement about where you are in the grief process and what you hope for yourself moving forward. Keep it with you and use it as motivation to continue the journey of healing.

References

Ackerman, C. E., MA. (2022, August 2). *10 Post Traumatic Growth (PTG) Worksheets & Practices.* PositivePsychology.com. https://positivepsychology.com/post-traumatic-growth-worksheets/

Ackerman, D. (1998). *A slender thread: Rediscovering hope at the heart of crisis.* Vintage Books.

Archer, J. (2008) Theories of grief: Past, present, and future perspectives. In M.S. Stroebe, T.O. Hansson, H. Schut, and W.Stroebe, *Handbook of bereavement research and practice: Advances in theory and intervention.* American Psychological Association.

Bansal, P., Bingemann, T. A., Greenhawt, M., Mosnaim, G., Nanda, A., Oppenheimer, J., Sharma, H., Stukus, D. and Shaker, M. (2020). Clinician wellness during the COVID-19 pandemic: extraordinary times and unusual challenges for the allergist/immunologist. *The Journal of Allergy and Clinical Immunology: In Practice, 8(6), 1781-1790.*

Beattie, M. (2006). *The grief club: The secret to getting through all kinds of change.* Hazelden.

Bellinger, W.H., Jr. (2012). *Psalms: A guide to studying the psalter* (2nd ed.). Baker Academic.

Biancalani, G., Azzola, C., Sassu, R., Marogna, C., & Testoni, I. (2022). Spirituality for coping with the trauma of a loved one's death during the covid-19 pandemic: An Italian qualitative study. *Pastoral Psychology.* Advance online publication. https://doi.org/10.1007/s11089-021-00989-8

Bidwell-Smith, C. (2018, October 2). *10 Ways to Overcome Grief-Related Anxiety.* Modern Loss. https://modernloss.com/10-ways-to-overcome-grief-related-anxiety/

Boelen, P. A., Olff, M., & Smid, G. E. (2019). Traumatic loss: Mental health consequences and implications for treatment and prevention. *European Journal of Psychotraumatology, 10(1), 1591331.* https://doi.org/10.1080/20008198.2019.1591331

Bonnano, G.A. (2019). *The other side of sadness: What the new science of bereavement tells us about life after loss.* Basic Books.

Bordere, T., Rheingold, A., and Williams, J. (2021). Grief following homicide. In Servaty-Seib, H. and Chapple, H.S. (Eds.), *Handbook of thanatology: The essential body of knowledge for the study of death, dying, and bereavement* (Third ed., 388-416). Association for Death Education and Counseling.

Breen, L.J., Szylit, R., Gilbert, K.R., Macpherson, C., Murphy, I., Nadeau, J.W., Resi e Silva, D., Wiegand, D.L., and International Work Group of Death, Dying, and Bereavement. (2019). Invitation to grief in the family context. *Death Studies* 43, (3), 173-182. https://doi.org/10.1080/0 7481187.2018.1442375

Bruggemann, W. (1995). *Psalms and the life of faith.* Augsburg Fortress.

Bruggemann, W. (1986). The costly loss of lament. *Journal for the Study of the Old Testament*, 36.

Cacciatore, J., Thieleman, K., Fretts, R., and Jackson, L.B. (2021, May 27). What is good grief support? Exploring the actors and actions in social support after traumatic grief. *PloS One,* 16(5), 1-17. https://doi.org/10.1371/journal.pone.0252324

Čepulienė, A. A., & Skruibis, P. (2022). The role of spirituality during suicide bereavement: a qualitative study. *International journal of environmental research and public health*, 19(14), 8740.

Clements, P.T., DeRanieri, J.T., Vigil, G.J., and Benasutti, K.M. (2004, October). Life after death: Grief therapy after the sudden traumatic death of a family member. *Perspectives in Psychiatric Care 40(4),* 149-154.

Coenen, C. (2020). *The creative toolkit for working with grief and bereavement: A practitioner's guide with activities and worksheets.* Jessica Kingsley Publishers.

Cowdry, T., & Stirling, J. (2020). Learnings from supporting traumatic grief in the aftermath of sudden epilepsy deaths. *Epilepsy & Behavior*, 103, 106416

Devine, M. (2021) *How to carry what can't be fixed: A journal for grief.* Sounds True.

Doka, K.J. and Chow, A.Y.M. (2021). Loss, grief, and mourning. In Servaty-Seib, H. and Chapple, H.S. (Eds.), *Handbook of thanatology: The essential body of knowledge for the study of death, dying, and bereavement* (Third ed., 235-261). Association for Death Education and Counseling.

Ellis, J.B. and Garske, G.G. (2007). Anishinabek Spirituality: Traversing Grief and Loss. *The International Journal of Diversity in Organizations, Communities, and Nations: Annual Review* 7(1): 229-236. doi:10.18848/1447-9532/CGP/v07i01/39306.

Gamino, L.A., Mowll, J., and Hogan, N.S. (2021). Grief following sudden nonvolitional deaths. In Servaty-Seib, H. and Chapple, H.S. (Eds.), *Handbook of thanatology: The essential body of knowledge for the study of death, dying, and bereavement* (Third ed., 336-361). Association for Death Education and Counseling.

Gilbert, K.R. and Macpherson, C. (2021). Contemporary grief theories. In Servaty-Seib, H. and Chapple, H.S. (Eds.), *Handbook of thanatology: The essential body of knowledge for the study of death, dying, and bereavement* (Third ed., 282-301). Association for Death Education and Counseling.

Gordin, Y. (2017). *Religion and Spirituality as Moderators in the Grief Experience.* [Unpublished doctoral dissertation]. The Chicago School of Professional Psychology.

Guinan, M.D. (2021, December 30). *Biblical laments: Prayer out of pain.* Franciscan Media. https://www.franciscanmedia.org/ ranciscan-spirit-blog/biblical-laments-prayer-out-of-pain/

Harris, C.B., Brookman, R., and O'Connor, M., (2021, October 22). It's not who you lose, it's who you are: Identity and symptom trajectory in prolonged grief. *Current Psychology*. https://doi.org/10.1007/s12144-021-02343-w

Hernandez, M.N. (2022). *Different after you: Rediscovering yourself and healing after grief and trauma.* New World Library.

Hicks, J.M. (2005). Preaching community laments: Responding to disillusionment with God and injustice in the world. *Performing the Psalms*, 67-81.

Igarashi, N., Aoyama, M., Ito, M., Nakajima, S., Sakaguchi, Y., Mmorita, T., Shima, Y. and Miyashita, M. (2021). Comparison of two measures for Complicated Grief: Brief Grief Questionnaire (BGQ) and Inventory of Complicated Grief (ICG). *Japanese Journal of Clinical Oncology*, 51(2), 252–257. Doi:10.1093/jjco/hyaa185

Jueckstock, J.A. (2018). Relational Spirituality and Grief: A Qualitative Analysis of Bereaved Parents. Journal of Psychology and Theology, 46(1), 38–51. https://doi.org/10.1177/0091647117753902

Kornfield, Jack. (2022, May 7). *Honoring Grief.* JackKornfield.com. https://jackkornfield.com/meditation-grief/

Lee, S. A., Gibbons, J. A., & Bottomley, J. S. (2022). Spirituality Influences Emotion Regulation During Grief Talk: The Moderating Role of Prolonged Grief Symptomatology. *Journal of Religion and Health,* 61(6), 4923-4933.

Lövgren M, Sveen J, Steineck G, Wallin AE, Eilertsen M-EB, Kreicbergs U (2019). Spirituality and religious coping are related to cancer-bereaved siblings' long-term grief. *Palliative and Supportive Care*, 17, 138–142. https://doi.org/10.1017/ S1478951517001146

Maass, U., Hofmann, L., Perlinger, J., & Wagner, B. (2022). Effects of bereavement groups–a systematic review and meta-analysis. *Death studies*, 46(3), 708-718. DOI: 10.1080/07481187.2020.1772410

Maccallum, F. and Bryant, R. (2018). Prolonged grief and attachment security: A latent class analysis. *Psychiatry Research*, 268, 297-302. https://doi.org/10.1016/j.psychres.2018.07.038

Maccallum, F. and Bryant, R.A. (2013). A cognitive attachment model of prolonged grief: Integrating attachments, memory, and identity. *Clinical Psychology Review* 33, 713-727.

Mangione, L., Lyons, M., & DiCello, D. (2016). Spirituality and religion in experiences of Italian American daughters grieving their fathers. *Psychology of Religion and Spirituality*, 8(3), 253–262. https://doi.org/10.1037/rel0000056

Masters, R.A. (2010). *Spiritual Bypassing*. North Atlantic Books.

McKendrick-Calder, L., Pollard, C., Shumka, C., McDonald, M., Carlson, S., & Winton, S. (2019). Mindful moments—enhancing deliberate practice in simulation learning. *Journal of Nursing Education*, 58(7), 431-431.

Mehdipour, F., Arefnia, R., and Szrei, E. (2020, June). Effects of Spiritual-Religion Interventions on Complicated Grief Syndrome and Psychological Hardiness of Mothers with Complicated Grief Disorder. *Health Spirituality and Medical Ethics*, 7(2), 20/26. DOI:10.29252/jhsme.7.2.20

Meichenbaum, D. (2012). *Roadmap to resilience: A guide for military, trauma victims and their families.* Institute Press. .

Milman, E., Neimeyer, R.A., and Boelen, P.A. (2021). Problematic grief. In Servaty-Seib, H. and Chapple, H.S. (Eds.), *Handbook of thanatology: The essential body of knowledge for the study of death, dying, and bereavement* (Third ed., 441-466). Association for Death Education and Counseling.

Milman, E., Neimeyer, R.A., Fitzpatrick, M., MacKinnon, C.J., Muis, K.R. and Cohen, S. R. (2017). Prolonged grief symptomatology following violent loss: the mediating role of meaning. *European Journal of Psychotraumatology* 8(1503522). https://doi.org/10.1080/20008198.2018.1503522© 2018

Mitchell, K.R. and Anderson, H. (1983). *All our losses, all our griefs: Resources for pastoral care.* Westminster John Knox Press.

Neff, K. (n.d.) Exercise 2: Self-compassion break. *Self-compassion.org.* https://self-compassion.org/exercise-2-self-compassion-break/

Neff, K. (n.d.) Exercise 3: Exploring self-compassion through writing. *Self-compassion.org.* https://self-compassion.org/exercise-3-exploring-self-compassion-writing/

Neimeyer, R.A., Milman, E.J., and Steffen, E.M. (2022). The meaning in loss group: Principles, processes and procedures. In Ed.Neimeyer, R.A. *New techniques of grief therapy: Bereavement and beyond* (26-45). Routledge.

Özcan, N. and Kaya, M. (2019). The effectiveness of Family Resiliency Program with traumatic grief on women's post-traumatic stress, grief, and family resiliency level. *Education and Science,* 44(197), 121-138. DOI: 10.15390/EB.2018.7663

Parkes, C.M. (1986). *Bereavement: Studies of grief in adult life.* Penguin Books.

Pennebaker, J. (2004). *Writing to heal: A guided journal for recovering from trauma & emotional upheaval.* New Harbinger Publications, Inc.

Phipps, C.B. (2018). Metamorphosis; An autoethnographic journey through loss, grief, and perceived identity changes. *Journal of Loss and Trauma,* 23(6), 458-467. https://doi.org/10.1080/15325024.2018.1475138

Pikörn, I. (n.d.). The 5-4-3-2-1 grounding technique: Manage anxiety by anchoring in the present. *Insight Timer Blog.* Insight Timer. https://insighttimer.com/blog/54321-grounding-technique/

Pone, L. (2017). *Resilient grieving: Finding strength and embracing life after a loss that changes everything.* The Experiment, LLC.

Prigerson, H.G., Kakarala, S., Gang, J. and Maciejewski, P.K. (2021). History and status of Prolonged Grief Disorder as a psychiatric diagnosis. *Annual Review of Clinical Psychology,* 17, 109-126.

Prigerson, H.G. and Maciejewski, P.L. (2018, January 2). Grief and acceptance as opposite sides of the same coin: setting a research agenda to study peaceful acceptance of loss. *British Journal of Psychiatry,* 193(6). https://www.cambridge.org/core/journals/the-british-journal-of-psychiatry/article/grief-and-acceptance-as-opposite-sides-of-the-same-coin-setting-a-research-agenda-to-study-peaceful-acceptance-of-loss/F3E88293BAC745834323E0A4D25CB318

Prigerson, H. G., Maciejewski, P. K., Reynolds, C. F., Bierhals, A. J., Newsom, J. T., Fasiczka, A., Frank, E., Doman, J., & Miller, M. (1995). Inventory of complicated grief: A scale to measure maladaptive symptoms of loss. *Psychiatry Research,* 59(1), 65–79. https://doi.org/10.1016/0165-1781(95)02757-2

Quality of Life Publishing Co. (2020). *Sudden loss*. Quality of Life Publishing Co.

Quality of Life Publishing Co. (2013) *When you are grieving*. Quality of Life Publishing Co.

Regehr, C., & Sussman, T. (2004). Intersections between grief and trauma: Toward an empirically based model for treating traumatic grief. *Brief Treatment & Crisis Intervention*, 4(3).

Reivich, K. (2020, June 1). *Foundations of positive psychology: Resilience skills in times of uncertainty*. (10 hour course on building resilience), University of Pennsylvania through Coursera.

Sanghvi, P. (2020). Grief in children and adolescents: A review. *Indian Journal of Mental Health*, 7(1), 6-14.

Schachter, S.R., Lee, G.L., and Fan, G. (2021). Grief following extended illness. In Servaty-Seib, H. and Chapple, H.S. (Eds.), *Handbook of thanatology: The essential body of knowledge for the study of death, dying, and bereavement* (Third ed., 308-335). Association for Death Education and Counseling.

Schenck, L., Eberle, K., and Rings, J. (2016). Insecure attachment styles and complicated grief severity: Applying what we know to inform future directions. *OMEGA Journal of Death and Dying*, 73(3), 231-249. DOI: 10.1177/0030222815576124

Schwartz, L.E., Howell, K.H., and Jamison, L.E. (2018). Effect of time since loss on grief, resilience, and depression among bereaved emerging adults. *Death Studies*, 42(9), 537-547. https://doi.org/10.10 80/07481187.2018.1430082

Smid, G.E. and Boelen, P.A. (2022). Culturally sensitive approaches to finding meaning in traumatic bereavement. In Ed. Neimeyer, R.A. *New techniques of grief therapy: Bereavement and beyond* (46-54). Routledge.

Smigelsky, M., Bottomley, J., Relyea, G. and Neimeyer, R. (2020). Investigating risk for grief severity: Attachment to the deceased and relationship quality. *Death Studies*, 44(7), 402-411. https://doi.or g/10.1080/07481187.2018.1548539

Soni, A. (2020. October 30). *What is spiritual bypassing: The dark side of spiritualism*. Calm Sage. https://www.calmsage.com/what-is-spiritual-bypassing/

Stang, H. (2021, January 7). Meditation for grief and sadness: A guided practice. *Mindfulness & Grief Institute*. https://mindfulnessandgrief.com/meditation-for-grief-and-sadness/

Stroebe, M. and Schut, H. (2010). The dual process model of coping with bereavement: A decade on. *OMEGA*, 61(4), 273-289.

Supiano, K.P. and Luptak, M. (2013). Complicated grief in older adults: A randomized controlled trial of complicated grief group therapy. *The Gerontologist* 54(5), 840–856. Doi:10.1093/geront/gnt076

Swenson, K.M. (2005). *Living through pain: Psalms and the search for wholeness*. Baylor University Press.

TheMindFool. (2021, February 17). *Spiritual bypassing: Does it help?* [Infographic]. Themindfool.com. https://themindfool.com/spiritual-bypassing/

Thomsen, D.K., Lundorff. M., Damkier, A., & O'Connor, M. (2018). Narrative identity and grief reactions: A prospective study of bereaved partners. *Journal of Applied Research in Memory and Cognition*, 7, 412-421.

Tolstikova, K., Fleming, S., and Chartier, B. (2005). Grief, complicated grief, and trauma: The role of the search for meaning, impaired self-reference, and death anxiety. *Illness, Crisis & Loss 13*(4), 293/313.

Wagner, B., Grafiadeli, R., Shäffer, T. and Hofmann, L. (2022, April). Efficacy of an online-group intervention after suicide bereavement: A randomized controlled trial. *Internet Interventions, 28.* https://doi.org/10.1016/j.invent.2022.100542

Waller, A., Turon, H., Mansfield, E., Clark, K., Hobden, B., & Sanson-Fisher, R. (2016). Assisting the bereaved: a systematic review of the evidence for grief counseling. *Palliative Medicine*, 30(2), 132-148. DOI:10.1177/0269216315588728

Williams, L. (2013, July 22). *Secondary loss—one loss isn't enough??!!*. Whatsyourgrief.com. https://whatsyourgrief.com/secondary-loss-one-loss-isnt-enough/

Williams, L. (2014, May 5). *Grief Work: the grief theory of Erich Lindemann*. Whatsyourgrief.com. https://whatsyourgrief.com/grief-work-grief-theory-erich-lindemann/

Wolfet, A.D. (2014). *Reframing PTSD as traumatic grief: How caregivers can companion traumatized grievers through catch-up mourning*. Companion Press.

Worden, J.W., Kosminsky, P., and Carverhill, P. (2021). Foundational grief theories. In Servaty-Seib, H. and Chapple, H.S. (Eds.), *Handbook of thanatology: The essential body of knowledge for the study of death, dying, and bereavement* (Third ed., 262-281). Association for Death Education and Counseling.

Wright, H.N. (2003) Grief—The tangled ball of emotions. *Teamvie.org.* https://www.teamevie.org/wp-content/uploads/2017/10/Tangled-Ball-of-Grief.pdf

Zampitella, C. Morse, R., and Easton, L.B. (2023, April 27). *Cultural humility applied: The role of faith and spirituality in clinical settings*. [A presentation on the importance of faith and spirituality in grief counseling]. Association for Death Education and Counseling 2023 Conference, Columbus, Ohio and virtual.

Zhai, Y. and Du, X. (2020). Loss and grief amidst COVID-19: A path to adaptation and resilience. *Brain, Behavior, and Immunity*, 87, 80-81. https://doi.org/10.1016/j.bbi.2020.04.053

About the Author

Cindy R. Wallace, BCC-SP, CCISM, CT, has worked as a chaplain for over twenty years, serving in hospitals, hospice, and mental health settings. She currently serves as the Mental Health Chaplain at the Washington D.C. VA Medical Center. Chaplain Wallace also serves as the DC VAMC's Co-chair of the Critical Incident Stress Management Team, Co-lead for the Suicide Postvention Team, and organizes and facilitates the site's veteran grief groups. She is an ordained minister in the Cooperative Baptist Fellowship and endorsed through CBF as a board-certified chaplain with a specialty in Suicide Prevention.

Made in the USA
Las Vegas, NV
12 December 2024

14079339R00059